Michael M. Dediu

Our Future Depends on Good World Education

Moving from frail education to solid education

DERC Publishing House
Tewksbury (Boston), Massachusetts, U. S. A.

Copyright ©2019 by Michael M. Dediu

All rights reserved

Published and printed in the
United States of America
On the Great Seal of the United States are included:
E Pluribus Unum (Out of many, one)
Annuit Coeptis (He has approved of the undertakings)
Novus Ordo Seclorum (New order of the ages)

Library of Congress Control Number: 2019915979

Dediu, Michael M.

Our Future Depends on Good World Education
Moving from frail education to solid education

ISBN-13: 978-1-950999-00-2

MSG0197341_SEGV4S4iGOrPfBk2eYUD
1-8156151641
1-3QVYMWT
1-3QVYMX0
06089D
26KR2BVM

Preface

It is well known that the over 7.7 B of people on Earth are, actually, just one very big family, with about 2.5 B of children under 18, and about 1.5 billion between 7 and 18, who, obviously, must go to school.

In order to have a **harmonious world, with Sustainable Peace, Freedom, Health, Friendship and Prosperity**, we do need a **Good World Education** for these over 1.5 billion children.

Right now the situation is far from good, and we present in this book some necessary changes.

Let's first remember a few excellent quotes:
As you sow, so shall you reap – from Latin: Ut sementem feceris ita metes.
Aristotle: The roots of education are bitter, but the fruit is sweet.
Plato: Ignorance, the root and stem of all evil.
Plato: No man should bring children into the world, who is unwilling to persevere to the end in their nature and education.
Plato: We ought to esteem it of the greatest importance, that the fictions, which children first hear, should be adapted in the most perfect manner to the promotion of virtue.
Beethoven: Recommend to your children virtue; that alone can make them happy, not gold. I speak from experience
Cicero: Cultivation to the mind is as necessary as food to the body.
Archimedes: There are things which seem incredible to most men who have not studied Mathematics.
Cicero: What nobler employment, or more valuable to the state, than that of the man who instructs the rising generation?

Yes, educating the world rising generation has a high priority, and in a harmonious world, will be done properly – this book gives clear and practical ideas.

Michael M. Dediu, Ph. D.
Tewksbury (Boston), U. S. A., 12 October 2019

Canada, Niagara Falls: Niagara SkyWheel in Dinosaur Park and Miniature Golf, near Clifton Hill and Oneida Lane, 1.5 km north of the Horseshoe Falls.

Table of Contents

Preface 3
Table of Contents 5
1 – 2.5 Billions 9
2- Four Levels of World Required Education 11
3 – Kindergarten: age 5 and 6 12
    L1.1 – World Language Mundo based on English for age 5 and 6 13
    L1.2 – Mathematics for age 5 and 6 15
    L1.3 – Science for age 5 and 6 16
    L1.4 – Computers for age 5 and 6 20
    L1.5 – Art & Practical Work for age 5 and 6 21
    L1.6 – World and local Geography for age 5 and 6 24
    L1.7 – World Citizenship for age 5 and 6 28
    L1.8 – World and local History of Peace for age 5 and 6 31
    L1.9 – World Classical Music for age 5 and 6 34
    L1.10 – Health & Physical Education for age 5 and 6 38
    L1.11 – Optional local language for age 5 and 6 39
4 – Primary (or elementary): age 7, 8, 9 and 10 40
    L2.1 – World Language Mundo based on English for age 7, 8, 9 and 10 41
    L2.2 – Mathematics for age 7, 8, 9 and 10 46
    L2.3 – Science & Medicine for age 7, 8, 9 and 10 48
    L2.4 – Computers for age 7, 8, 9 and 10 52

L2.5 – Art & Practical Work for age 7, 8, 9 and 10 53

L2.6 – World and local Geography for age 7, 8, 9 and 10 56

L2.7 – World Citizenship & Economics for age 7, 8, 9 and 10 60

L2.8 – World and local History of Peace for age 7, 8, 9 and 10 63

L2.9 – World Classical Music for age 7, 8, 9 and 10 68

L2.10 – Health, Physical Education & Civilized Sport for age 7, 8, 9 and 10 73

L2.11 – Optional local or other language for age 7, 8, 9 and 10 76

5 – Secondary: age 11, 12 and 13 77

L3.1 – World Language Mundo based on English for age 11, 12 and 13 78

L3.2 – Mathematics for age 11, 12 and 13 82

L3.3 – Science & Medicine for age 11, 12 and 13 85

L3.4 – Computers & Technology for age 11, 12 and 13 88

L3.5 – Art & Practical Work for age 11, 12 and 13 90

L3.6 – World and local Geography for age 11, 12 and 13 95

L3.7 – World Citizenship & Economics for age 11, 12 and 13 100

L3.8 – World and local History of Peace for age 11, 12 and 13 102

L3.9 – World Classical Music for age 11, 12 and 13 105

L3.10 – Health, Physical Education & Civilized Sport for age 11, 12 and 13 111

L3.11 – Optional local or other language for age 11, 12 and 13 113

6 – High School or Vocational: age 14, 15, 16 and 17 115

L4.1 – World Language Mundo based on English for age 14, 15, 16 and 17 116

L4.2 – Mathematics for age 14, 15, 16 and 17 120

L4.3 – Science & (Medicine or Nursing) for age 14, 15, 16 and 17 ... 123

L4.4 – Computers & (Technology or Vocational 1) for age 14, 15, 16 and 17 128

L4.5 – (Art & Practical Work) or Vocational 2 for age 14, 15, 16 and 17 133

L4.6 – Business collaboration for age 14, 15, 16 and 17 139

L4.7 – World Citizenship & (Economics or Vocational 3) for age 14, 15, 16 and 17 141

L4.8 – Advanced Mathematics or Vocational 4 for age 14, 15, 16 and 17 147

L4.9 – Advanced Science or Vocational 5 for age 14, 15, 16 and 17 151

L4.10 – Health, Physical Education & Civilized Sport for age 14, 15, 16 and 17 156

L4.11 – Optional other language for age 14, 15, 16 and 17 158

7 – Education at all levels 159

8 – Science and Technology 163

9 - World Constitution 166

10 - Conclusions 168

Bibliography 170

Japan, Tokyo (1150): In Shinjuku, Shinjuku Center Bldg (223 m, 54 fl, 1979, left), Mode Gakuen Cocoon Tower (204 m, 50 fl, 2008, center-left), Keio Plaza Hotel North Tower (180 m, 47 fl, 1971, center-right).

1 – 2.5 Billions

1- The over 7.7 billions (or milliards, which is very common in most other European languages, like Bulgarian, Catalan, Croatian, Czech, Danish, Dutch, Finnish, French, Georgian, German, Hungarian, Italian, Norwegian, Polish, Portuguese, Romanian, Russian, Serbian, Slovak, Spanish and Swedish) of people on Earth are, actually, just one very big family, with about 2.5 billions of children under 18, and about 1.5 billion between 7 and 18, who, obviously, must go to school. As I mentioned, in order to have a harmonious world, with Sustainable Peace, Freedom, Health, Friendship and Prosperity, we do need a Good World Education for these 1.5 billion children. Right now the situation is far from good, and we present in this book some necessary changes.

Italy, Venezia - Libreria Sansoviniana (left), Il Campanile (center-left), Palazzo Ducale (right), and a Japanese couple wedding picture.

The biggest countries by population are: 1 China (1,433 Millions). 2 India (1,366 M), 3 United States (329 M), 4 Indonesia

(270 M), 5 Pakistan (216 M), 6 Brazil (211 M), 7 Nigeria (200 M), 8 Bangladesh (163 M), 9 Russia (145 M), 10 Mexico (127 M).

Between the smallest countries by population are: 233 (smallest) Vatican City (799), 217 San Marino (33,860), 216 Liechtenstein (38,019), 214 Monaco (38,964), 203 Andorra (77,142).

World Centers for Education Research and Support should change location every year, with the assistance of the United Nations, and could start, for example, in Shanghai, Mumbai, New York City, Surabaya, Karachi, Sao Paulo, Lagos, Chittagong, Saint Petersburg, Ecatepec (Mexico), Hamhung (North Korea), Zurich, Dubai, Iasi, Bo (Sierra Leone), and Vatican City.

UK, London: On Bow St, Royal Opera House at Covent Garden (1732, 1808, 1858, 1999, capacity 2,256). In 1734, Covent Garden presented its first ballet, Pygmalion.

2- Four Levels of World Required Education

2- The world needs 4 levels of education:
L1 – Kindergarten – 2 years: age 5 and 6
L2 – Primary School – 4 years: age 7, 8, 9 and 10
L3 – Secondary School – 3 years: age 11, 12 and 13
L4 – High School or Vocational School – 4 years: age 14, 15, 16 and 17

World Centers for each of these 4 Levels of Education should change location every year, with the assistance of the United Nations, and could start, for example, in Washington, Beijing, Moscow, London, Paris, New Delhi, Islamabad, Jerusalem, Tokyo, Berlin, Rome, Pyongyang, Seoul, Abuja, Brasilia, Damascus, Kiev, Aden, Tripoli, and Vaduz.

Italy, Milano, 30 Sep 2008, in Piazza della Scala, looking east to the statue (1872, by Pietro Magni) of Leonardo da Vinci (1452-1519), Banca Commerciale Italiana Palace (left, 1910), Palazzo Marino (right, 1557-1563, for Tommaso Marino (1475-1572 banker)).

3 – Kindergarten: age 5 and 6

3 - The subjects for the Level 1 Kindergarten:
L1.1 – World Language Mundo based on English
L1.2 – Mathematics
L1.3 – Science
L1.4 – Computers
L1.5 – Art & Practical Work
L1.6 – World and local Geography
L1.7 – World Citizenship
L1.8 – World and local History of Peace
L1.9 – World Classical Music
L1.10 – Health & Physical Education
L1.11 – Optional local language

Now we will give some details about each of these subjects.

Canada, Niagara Falls: Niagara SkyWheel in Dinosaur Park and Miniature Golf, near Clifton Hill and Oneida Lane, 1.5 km north of the Horseshoe Falls.

L1.1 – World Language Mundo based on English for age 5 and 6

- Explain and start to learn the alphabet
- Speaking Mundo
- Vocabulary development
- Using only peace-oriented kindergarten books in Mundo (or English)

Recommended books (especially for their pictures, because of the kindergarten level) from the Bibliography of this book:
- Venice (Venezia) – a new perspective. A short presentation with photographs
- La Serenissima (Venice) - a new photographic perspective. A short presentation with many photos
- Grand Canal – Venice. A new photographic viewpoint. A short presentation with many photos
- Rome, Boston and Helsinki. A short photographic presentation
- London and Greenwich, A photographic documentary

UK, London: From Newington Butts, in front of the entrance to the Elephant and Castle Shopping Centre, a small statue Elephant and Castle, and a tall building (left back) with 3 horizontal holes on top.

In this photo we see a small bridge on the street Riva dei Sette Martiri, on the south-east part of Venice, about 1 km south-est of Piazza San Marco, and very close to Giardini Pubblici and La Biennale di Venezia, which are on the right, after those threes. Also, to the right there are Fondamenta San Giuseppe and Viale Trento. Behind the second building there are Calle San Domenico Dorsoduro and Viale Giuseppe Garibaldi, both perpendicular on Fondamenta San Giuseppe.

Giardini Pubblici (Public Gardens), created under Napoleon, have palm trees, acacias, plane trees, and numerous statues and viewpoints over the Venetian lagoon. The lavish green of the park is surrounded by the walls, canals and stone buildings of Venice. Since La Biennale was founded, the exhibition pavilions of different countries are presented here. The pavilions' different styles are to be appreciated, because they range from the Gründerzeit in the 19th century (the Russian pavilion), to Classicism (the Italian Pavilion).

L1.2 – Mathematics for age 5 and 6

- usual kindergarten mathematics, including
- number recognition,
- counting skills,
- basic addition and subtraction,
- money counting, and similar subjects.

Recommended books from the Bibliography of this book:
- Newton, Benjamin Franklin, and Gauss, A chronological and photographic documentary

6 April 1978, Pisa, Cattedrale di Pisa (1092, striped-marble, left), Torre di Pisa (August 1173-1372, 55.86 m on the low side, 56.67 m on the high side, white-marble, 296 steps, right).

L1.3 – Science for age 5 and 6

Usual kindergarten science, including:
- My body
- Weather
- Describe objects in terms of the materials that make them up (cloth, paper, wood, etc.)
- The life cycle of a butterfly
- Describe the physical properties of objects (color, shape, texture, etc.)
- Balloon rocket
- Light, reflections and refraction, and the way the human eye works.
- Describe objects in terms of whether they float, sink, are attracted to magnets, etc.
- Grow your own bean plants
- The Sun, Moon, temperature, and melting
- LEGO construction
- Learning about the world and how it works
- World Space Week – celebrating science and technology – in the second week of October. It should be extended for many more weeks.

Recommended books (for their pictures) from the Bibliography of this book:
- Venice (Venezia) – a new perspective. A short presentation with photographs
- Rome and Tokyo – two captivating cities. A short photographic presentation
- Discover America and Japan - A photographic documentary
- Pythagoras to Fermi: History of Science - A chronological and photographic documentary

USA, San Francisco (1776), the northeast part of the Golden Gate Park (1870, 4.1 km^2), the Conservatory of Flowers (1876, 1879, 1995, Italian and Gothic architecture, houses a collection of rare and exotic plants, the oldest existing public conservatory in the western hemisphere), 22 Dec. 2014. This first greenhouse was completed in 1879. It was patterned after the Conservatory Kew Gardens, England, a distinguished example of late Victorian style, using early techniques of mass production and assembly of simple glass units.

In this picture, on the left, there is Biblioteca Servizio Didattico Universita Ca' Foscari (The Library for the Professors of the University Ca' Foscari).

Ca' Foscari University has about 20,000 enrolled students, with a wide range of subjects in four main areas: economics, languages, sciences and humanities. The University offers First Cycle Degree Programmes and Second Cycle Degree Programmes, over 25 Specialist Master's Programmes and 15 Research Doctorates. Ca' Foscari also offers Summer Schools, including the esteemed Ca' Foscari - Harvard Summer School, the result of an arrangement between Ca' Foscari and the American university

USA, Washington, D.C. (1790) in 2007: a Lunar module in The National Air and Space Museum (1976) of the Smithsonian Institution.

UK, London: Near the Buckingham Palace (1703, 1850, 1913), a traditional horse (Cleveland Bay) drawn carriage (Clarence (Brougham), 1810 style).

L1.4 – Computers for age 5 and 6

- Computer parts names
- How to use a computer
- Playing with a computer
- Computer games

Recommended books from the Bibliography of this book:
- From Euclid to Edison - revelries in the last 75 years - A chronological and photographic documentary

Italy: Venezia in 2012: Piazzetta dei Leoncini, on the north side of the Basilica di San Marco, with two marble lions (offered by Doge Alvise Mocenigo in 1722).

L1.5 – Art & Practical Work for age 5 and 6

- Classical paintings and sculptures
- Learning to use some painting tools, etc.
- Drawing
- Self-care
- Cooking
- Flower arranging
- Plant care
- LEGO building
- Prepare gifts

Recommended books from the Bibliography of this book:
- The City of Light – Paris (La Ville-Lumière) - A kaleidoscopic photographic presentation
- 200 Wonderful Places, In The Last 50 Years – A personal photographic documentary

Japan, Nikko, (140 km north of Tokyo, with 103 shrines and temples): statue inside Nakajinko (1646, storehouse building), part of Tosho-gu shrine (1636, 42 buildings).

France, Paris: The statue l'Hiver (1702) by Jean Raon (1631 – 1707), placed in 1722 on the east side of the Basin Octogonal in Jardin des Tuileries (created in 1564 as the garden of Palais des Tuileries (1564 – 1883, which was located between le Pavillon de Marsan, at the west end of the north part of Musée du Louvre, and Pavillon de Flore, at the west end of the south part of Musée du Louvre)).

Japan, Osaka, very nice flower arrangement coming from a basket, near the north side of the Osaka Castle (1597).

UK, London: From the northwest corner of Trafalgar Square (1840), looking northeast to The National Gallery (1824, over 2,300 paintings, left), St. Martin in the Fields Church (1724, right, with music recitals).

L1.6 – World and local Geography for age 5 and 6

- Globes and maps
- Continents
- Oceans
- Mountains
- Rivers
- Roads
- Bridges
- Cities
- Parks
- Canals

Recommended books (for their pictures) from the Bibliography of this book:
- Venice (Venezia) – a new perspective. A short presentation with photographs
- From Niagara Falls to Mount Fuji via Rome - A novel photographic presentation
- London and Greenwich, A photographic documentary

USA, 11 July 2009, tall ship at the northwest side of Boston Fish Pier in Boston (1630, population 650,000) Harbor (Port of Boston has 200 ha, draft depth 12 m, 237,000 containers/year; the Boston Harbor walk provides public access to much of the harbor's edge).

This picture shows the most famous place in Venice, Italy, and one of the most beautiful squares in the world – Piazza San Marco, a real marble meeting place. The west façade of Basilica di San Marco, with its great arches and marble decorations, is in the back, il Campanile (the Bell Tower) on the right, Torre dell'Orologio, completed in 1499, is on the left back, Procuratie Vecchie, the old procuracies, built around 1520, are on the left, and Procuratie Nuove on the right.

UK, London: From a boat on Thames (flowing left to right), looking southwest to the Westminster Bridge (1862, 250 m), the east (left) and north sides of Palace of Westminster (1016, 1870), Big Ben (1855, 96 m, right).

La belle ferronnière, 1490, by Leonardo da Vinci

L1.7 – World Citizenship for age 5 and 6

- World
- One big family
- Follow rules
- Discipline
- Respect your parents and others
- Trustworthy
- Volunteer
- Honesty
- Modesty
- Help others
- Take responsibility for your actions
- Be informed
- Be compassionate
- Be a good neighbor
- Do not make noise
- Be polite
- Speak nicely

Recommended books from the Bibliography of this book:
- Rome, Boston and Helsinki. A short photographic presentation
- Beautiful Places on Earth – A new photographic presentation
- Paris (Lutetia Parisiorum) – the romance capital of the world - A kaleidoscopic photographic view
- Our Future is Sustainable Peace and Prosperity – Moving from conflicts to harmony and peace

USA, New York, on 1st Ave, the northwest façade of the building for the headquarters of the United Nations (1948-1952, 155 m, 39 floors, 193 nations). The main headquarters in New York City contains the seats of the principal organs of the UN, including the General Assembly and Security Council.

Finland, Helsinki: The Swedish Theatre (in Swedish Svenska Teatern) is a Swedish-speaking theatre in Helsinki, located at the central Erottaja square, at the west end of the attractive Esplanadi park. It was the first national stage of Finland, built in 1860 and renovated in 1866 and 1935.

France, Paris: Mannequins representing Gustave Eiffel (right, 57 years old) talking in 1889 to Thomas Edison (left, 42 years old) in Eiffel's apartment in Tour Eiffel (1889, 324 m).

L1.8 – World and local History of Peace for age 5 and 6

- Antiquity and peace
- Middle Ages and peace
- Modern time and peace

Recommended books (for their pictures) from the Bibliography of this book:
- Venice (Venezia) – a new perspective. A short presentation with photographs
- From America to Switzerland via France - A photographic documentary
- World History, a new perspective - A chronological and photographic documentary

USA, The Chinese Tea House (1150 Song Dynasty temple style) on the eastern end, near the ocean, of the backyard of Marble House, 1888-1892, William Kissam Vanderbilt (1849-1920), and his wife Alva.

La bella Venezia, the beautiful Venice, with its inimitable Venetian Gothic style, is one of the most beautiful, famous and visited cities in the world, and is sited on 118 small islands, located in the marshy Venetian Lagoon, between the mouths of the Po and the Piave Rivers.

This picture shows, on Monday October 22, 2012, at 9 AM, the south façade and a part of the east façade of Palazzo Ducale (Doge's Palace), which is situated on the south-east corner of Piazza San Marco. This Palazzo, which is more than 600 years old and took other 600 years to build it, was started around 820, then reconstructed several times, and finally finished, around 1420. Its facades have a total length of approximately 152 m, and date from circa 1309 - 1424. Down can be seen a bridge on the street Riva degli Schiavoni. From this bridge one can see Il Ponte dei Sospiri.

UK, Cambridge: From the King's Parade, looking southwest to the east façade of the entrance of King's College (1441, by King Henry VI (1421-1471)).

Rome: Accademia Nazionale dei Lincei (1603) in Villa Farnesina (1510). The author was invited to give a lecture here in 1977.

L1.9 – World Classical Music for age 5 and 6

- Listening to Mozart, Vivaldi, Bach, Hayden, Verdi, Rossini, etc.
- Musical instruments
- Singing together
- Mathematics and music

Recommended books (for their pictures) from the Bibliography of this book:
- Venice (Venezia) – a new perspective. A short presentation with photographs
- The City of Light – Paris (La Ville-Lumière) - A kaleidoscopic photographic presentation
- Vivaldi, Bach, Mozart, and Verdi, A chronological and photographic documentary
- Sutherland to Pavarotti: Great Singers History - A chronological and photographic documentary

Italia - 23 October 2009, Trieste (177 BC part of the Roman Republic), from Passo Fausto Pecorari, in Piazza San Giovanni, looking southeast to the statue of Giuseppe Verdi (1813-1901), and buildings on Via Giacinto Gallina (left) and Via delle Torri (right).

This picture displays Terminal S. Basilio, Venice, Italy, a smaller cruise terminal, for smaller ships. In the center of the picture, there is a nice sculpture with three musicians playing a contrabass, a violin, and a clarinet.

France, Paris: The central part of the façade of L'Opéra de Paris (1875): composers Daniel Auber (1782–1871, left), Ludwig van Beethoven (1770–1827, second), Wolfgang Amadeus Mozart (1756–1791, center) and Gaspare Spontini (1774–1851, right).

On the façade of l'Opéra de Paris (1875): a statue and the bust of Franz Joseph Haydn (1732 – 1809), prolific and important Austrian Composer. He signed his musical work in Italian: "di me giuseppe Haydn" (by me Joseph Haydn). He wrote a great number of concertos, masses, operas, piano trios, solo piano compositions, string quartets, symphonies, baritone trios, and Gott erhalte Franz den Kaiser, which was used in Das Lied der Deutschen – Germany's national anthem.

Italy, Trieste, 23 Oct 2009, inside Teatro Verdi, commemoration dedicated to Claudio Monteverdi (1567-1643, composer, gambist, singer, and Catholic priest). He wrote 9 books of Madrigali (1587-1643, the ninth book was published posthumously in 1651), 18 operas, but only L'Orfeo (1609), Il ritorno d'Ulisse in patria (1640), L'incoronazione di Poppea (1642), and the famous aria, Lamento, from his second opera L'Arianna (1608), have survived, and sacred music (Vespro della Beata Vergine (1610), Messa in illo tempore (1610), Mass of Thanksgiving (1631), Messa a 4 da Cappela(1641), and others). Monteverdi developed two styles of composition – the heritage of Renaissance polyphony and the new basso continuo technique of the Baroque. He wrote one of the earliest operas, *L'Orfeo*, that is the earliest surviving opera still regularly performed.

L1.10 – Health & Physical Education for age 5 and 6

- Self-care
- Washing
- Good food
- Dental care
- Stay clean
- Self discipline
- Be optimist
- Gymnastics
- Ball play
- Circle play
- Running
- Jumping
- Dance

Recommended books from the Bibliography of this book:
- Hippocrates to Fleming: Medicine History celebrated after 1943 - A chronological and photographic documentary

UK, Greenwich: The meridian 0 (Prime meridian, 1851, official 1884, stainless steel strip under the man in red), Flamsteed House (1676, center up).

L1.11 – Optional local language for age 5 and 6

If a school is in China, for example, the parents could choose Chinese or Italian for their children.

Recommended books from the Bibliography of this book:
- Da Vinci, Michelangelo, Rembrandt, Rodin - A chronological and photographic documentary

Michelangelo

4 – Primary (or elementary): age 7, 8, 9 and 10

4 – The subjects for the Level 2 Primary or Elementary:
L2.1 – World Language Mundo based on English
L2.2 – Mathematics
L2.3 – Science & Medicine
L2.4 – Computers
L2.5 – Art & Practical Work
L2.6 – World and local Geography
L2.7 – World Citizenship & Economics
L2.8 – World and local History of Peace
L2.9 – World Classical Music
L2.10 – Health, Physical Education & Civilized Sport
L2.11 – Optional local or other language

Italy, Rome (753 BC), Villa Borghese (1630), Lake Garden, from Viale del Lago, Tempio di Esculapio (1786, Temple of Asclepius (god of medicine, healing, rejuvenation and physicians)) on artificial island; on front, in Greek "To Asclepius the savior".

L2.1 – World Language Mundo based on English for age 7, 8, 9 and 10

- Reading in Mundo
- Speaking only Mundo
- Writing in Mundo
- Grammar
- Examples
- Vocabulary development
- Practice
- Using only peace-oriented books in Mundo (or English)

Recommended books from the Bibliography of this book:
- Venice (Venezia) – a new perspective. A short presentation with photographs
- La Serenissima (Venice) - a new photographic perspective. A short presentation with many photos
- Discover America and Japan - A photographic documentary
- Vergilius, Horatius, Ovidius, and Shakespeare, A chronological and photographic documentary
- Socrates to Churchill - Aphorisms celebrated after 1960 - A chronological and photographic documentary

USA, Boston (1629, motto: Sicut patribus sit Deus nobis (As God was with our fathers, so may He be with us), the capital and largest city of Massachusetts, with the first US public school, Boston Latin School (1635), and first subway system (1897), international center of higher education, medicine and innovation), 20 June 2015, Boston Public Garden (1837, 9.7 ha, 1 km south of MGH, adjacent to the Boston Common), the statue of Edward Everett Hale (1822 – 1909, Man of Letters, Patriot, minister) by Beta Pratt in 1869.

Italy, Venice: On a bridge in the south of Murano, Fondamenta Daniele Manin (right), Fondamenta dei Vetrai (left), looking northeast, towards the center of Murano.

Canada, Niagara Falls: the American Falls (21-30 m drop, 290 m wide, left), and the Horseshoe Falls (in Canada, 53 m drop, 790 m wide, right), with a boat with tourists and an amazing rainbow.

Slovenia, 2 Nov 2009, statue of France Preseren (1800-1849, educated at the University of Vienna, the greatest Slovene poet), at Cyril and Methodius Square, in Ljubljana (80 km northeast of Trieste).

USA, 3 Dec 2009, from Avenue Louis Pasteur (1822-1895, French microbiologist), Boston Public Latin School (1635, Schola Latina Bostoniensis, the oldest and the first public exam school in the US).

Statue of Ovidius in Constanta, Romania. Ovidius, in 8 AD, suddenly was sent personally by Augustus, 71, into exile to Tomis (now Constanta, Romania) in the eastern province Scythila Minor, on the Black Sea, where he remained until his death in 17.

L2.2 – Mathematics for age 7, 8, 9 and 10

- usual elementary mathematics, including
- numeration
- arithmetic
- geometry
- algebra
- measurement

Recommended books from the Bibliography of this book:
- From Berkeley to Pompeii via Rome – A kaleidoscopic photographic documentary
- Newton, Benjamin Franklin, and Gauss, A chronological and photographic documentary

Italy, Trieste, 22 Oct 2009, in Piazza Giuseppe Verdi, looking north to Teatro Lirico Giuseppe Verdi (1813-1901). with Stagione sinfonica 2009, which includes Mozart (1756-1791), Haydn (1732-1809), Paganini (1782-1840), von Weber (1786-1826), and Respighi (1879-1936).

USA, the University of California, Berkeley (1868, named after the philosopher and mathematician Bishop George Berkeley (1685-1753), motto Fiat lux (Let there be light), 36,200 students, major public research university, 72 Nobel laureates, between the top six universities in the world, 500 ha campus), il Campanile (Sather Tower (61 bells (full concert carillon) and clock tower). 1914, 94 m, 7 floors, observation deck on the 8th floor, inspired by il Campanile (850, 1514, 1912, 99 m) di San Marco (1084), Venezia (421, Venice), Italy (900 BC)).

L2.3 – Science & Medicine for age 7, 8, 9 and 10

Usual primary science and medicine including:
- The body
- Healthy living habits
- Personal hygiene
- Food
- Air
- Weather
- Plants and animals
- The life cycle
- Balloon rocket
- Light, reflections and refraction, and the way the human eye works.
- Grow your own bean plants
- The Sun, Moon, temperature, and melting
- Chemical reactions
- LEGO construction
- Learning about the world and how it works
- World Space Week – celebrating science and technology – in the second week of October. It should be extended for many more weeks.

Recommended books from the Bibliography of this book:
- Rome and Tokyo – two captivating cities. A short photographic presentation
- 200 Wonderful Places, In The Last 50 Years – A personal photographic documentary
- Newton, Benjamin Franklin, and Gauss, A chronological and photographic documentary
- Hippocrates to Fleming: Medicine History celebrated after 1943 - A chronological and photographic documentary
- Pythagoras to Fermi: History of Science - A chronological and photographic documentary

Japan, Tsukuba: A reconstruction of Aucasaurus garridoi, a ceratosaurian medium-sized theropod dinosaurus, which lived during the Santonian stage (about 85 million years ago), in a Museum in Tsukuba Science City (1962), in Ibaraki Prefecture, 60 km north-east of Tokyo.

USA, Washington (1790) in 2007: Smithsonian National Museum of Natural History (1910, wings added in the 1960s, 126 millions of objects), on the National Mall, on Constitution Avenue NW.

USA, Washington, D.C. (1790): the 1903 Wright Flyer airplane, at The National Air and Space Museum (1976) of the Smithsonian Institution, between Jefferson Dr SW and Independence Ave SW.

UK, Greenwich: On the south side of the Royal Observatory, with the meridian 0 being in the middle between the two white vertical lines (right), a part of a 12 m reflecting telescope, built in 1789 for the astronomer William Herschel (1738-1822, discovered Uranus in 1781).

UK, Oxford: Inside Weston Library, part of the Bodleian Libraries of the University of Oxford, Louis Pasteur (1822-1895) and Robert Koch (1843-1910), with milestones of discovery and innovation.

Switzerland: from Genève to Thoiry (France), on Route de Meyrin, 2 km west from Geneva Cointrin Airport, there is this renovation of the external structural Elements of the Globe of Science and Innovation.

L2.4 – Computers for age 7, 8, 9 and 10

- Computer parts names
- How to use a computer
- Beginning to use a computer for practical applications
- Word processing
- E-mail
- Spreadsheets
- Internet
- Computer games

Recommended books from the Bibliography of this book:
- From Euclid to Edison - revelries in the last 75 years - A chronological and photographic documentary
- Archimedes to Ford: Invention History celebrated after 1943 - A chronological and photographic documentary

Australia, Sydney (1788, 5 M people), from the Royal Botanic Gardens looking to the southeast side of the harbourfront Sydney Opera House (1959-1973, 183 m by 120 m by 65 m height, total seating capacity 5738)) and the Sydney Harbour Bridge (1932, left).

L2.5 – Art & Practical Work for age 7, 8, 9 and 10

- Classical paintings and sculptures
- Learning to use some painting tools, etc.
- Drawing
- Painting
- Self-care
- Cooking
- Ceramics
- Printmaking
- LEGO building
- Prepare gifts

Recommended books from the Bibliography of this book:
- La Serenissima (Venice) - a new photographic perspective. A short presentation with many photos
- From USA to Japan via Canada – A cheerful photographic documentary

Italy, Venice, Murano: Detail of a shop window with artistic Murano glass.

Paris: The western façade of Cathédrale Notre Dame de Paris (1163 – 1345, 90 m), on the south-eastern part of the Île de la Cité, which is considered the center of Paris, in the fourth arrondissement. The three Portals are: Portal of the Virgin, Portal of the Last Judgment, and Portal of St-Anne. The organ has 7,374 pipes, with about 900 classified as historical. It has 110 real stops, five 56-key manuals and a 32-key pedalboard; it is now fully computerized.

Japan: A gorgeous classical bronze sculpture on a street in Sendai (1600, 300 km north-east of Tokyo), the largest city in the Tohoku Region and one of the country's fifteen largest cities, with about one million inhabitants. Sendai is the capital city of Miyagi Prefecture.

L2.6 – World and local Geography for age 7, 8, 9 and 10

- Globes and maps
- Continents
- Oceans
- Mountains
- Rivers
- Roads
- Bridges
- Cities
- Parks
- Canals
- Comparing, describing

Recommended books from the Bibliography of this book:
- La Serenissima (Venice) - a new photographic perspective. A short presentation with many photos
- From Niagara Falls to Mount Fuji via Rome - A novel photographic presentation
- From the USA and Canada to Italy and Japan - A fresh photographic presentation
- The City of Light – Paris (La Ville-Lumière) - A kaleidoscopic photographic presentation
- Paris and Tokyo – a joyful photographic presentation. With a preamble about the Universe

Italy, Venezia: Costa Fascinosa cruise ship passing south of Piazza San Marco.

Niagara Falls (8000 BC, the highest flow rate in the world), with the American Falls (left down), the Horseshoe Falls (left up, Canada, 53 m drop, 790 m wide), Niagara Falls city (center, Canada), and an American boat (left) and a Canadian boat (right).

Tokyo Skytree - a broadcasting, restaurant, and observation tower located in Sumida, Tokyo. It became the tallest structure in Japan in 2010 and reached its full height of 634 m in March 2011, making it the tallest tower in the world, and the second tallest structure in the world. The tower opened to the public on 22 May 2012. Without antenna it is 495 m, top observation floor-is at 451.2 m, and the second observation floor is at 350 m. It has 13 elevators. The exterior lattice is painted a color called "Skytree White". This is an original color based on a bluish white traditional Japanese color (aijiro). The tower is illuminated using LED lights.

Italy, Milano, 30 Sep 2008, in Piazza del Duomo, looking southeast to the north side of il Duomo (Basilica cattedrale metropolitana di Santa Maria Nascente, 1386-1965 (579 years), capacity 40,000, length 158.5 m, width 92 m, maximum height 108 m, 135 spires, materials: brick and Candoglia marble, architects: Donato Bramante (1444-1514), Leonardo da Vinci (1452-1519), Giulio Romano (1499-1546), Pellegrino Tibaldi (1527-1596)). On May 20, 1805, Napoleon Bonaparte (1769-1821), about to be crowned King of Italy, ordered the façade to be finished by Pellicani. For this, a statue of Napoleon was placed at the top of one of the spires. Napoleon was crowned King of Italy at the Duomo on May 26, 1805.

L2.7 – World Citizenship & Economics for age 7, 8, 9 and 10

- World
- One big family
- Follow rules
- Discipline
- Respect your parents and others
- Trustworthy
- Volunteer
- Honesty
- Modesty
- Help others
- Take responsibility for your actions
- Be informed
- Be compassionate
- Be a good neighbor
- Do not make noise
- Be polite
- Speak nicely
- World Constitution
- Examples

- Work and Profit
- Finance
- Utility
- Individual Wealth
- World Wealth

Recommended books from the Bibliography of this book:
- Beautiful Places on Earth – A new photographic presentation
- Paris (Lutetia Parisiorum) – the romance capital of the world - A kaleidoscopic photographic view
Our Future is Sustainable Peace and Prosperity – Moving from conflicts to harmony and peace

USA, Washington, D.C. (founded 1790) United States Capitol (1793 – 1800, 88 m), seen from the west, near the Reflecting Pool

Italy, the entrance to the modern city of Pompei, located southeast of the ruins of the ancient Pompeii (650 BC, in 79 covered by ash).

France, La Monnaie de Paris (the Direction of Coins and Medals) created in 864 by Charles II (823-877, king 843-877), is the oldest French institution, which is still active. It also has a Musée de la Monnaie (1833), at 11 Quai de Conti, in the 6th arrondissement.

L2.8 – World and local History of Peace for age 7, 8, 9 and 10

- Antiquity and peace
- Middle Ages and peace
- Modern time and peace
- Examples
- Analysis

Recommended books from the Bibliography of this book:
- Rome, Boston and Helsinki. A short photographic presentation
- Paris (Lutetia Parisiorum) – the romance capital of the world - A kaleidoscopic photographic view
- World History, a new perspective - A chronological and photographic documentary

France, Paris: Children having a class of history on Ave. de la Grande Armée (left) at Place Charles de Gaulle (1890-1970), near l'Arc de Triomphe de l'Étoile (1836, started by Napoleon in 1806, 50 m).

USA, Boston: From One Marina Park Drive building on Boston Fan Pier, looking south-east to South Boston Harbor: Logan International Airport (left up), Seaport World Trade Center (center left), the Institute of Contemporary Art (left down), and many waterfront tall buildings on the right.

Since its discovery by John Smith in 1614, Boston Harbor has been a vital port in American history. It was the site of many historical events, like the Boston Tea Party (which was a political protest, on December 16, 1773, by throwing the tea into Boston Harbor, by the Sons of Liberty in Boston, then in the British colony of Massachusetts, against the tax policy of the British government and the East India Company, that controlled all the tea imported into the colonies), as well as almost continuous backfilling of the harbor until the 19th century. By 1660 almost all imports came to the greater Boston area and the New England coast through the waters of Boston Harbor. A fast arrival of people transformed Boston into a prosperous city.

Italy: Roma in 2011: Fontana della Barcaccia by Gian Lorenzo Bernini, 1623, in Piazza di Spagna, below the Scalinata della Trinità dei Monti (the Spanish Steps, Francisco de Sanctis, 1725, left).

Washington, D.C. (1790) in 2007: National Archives and Records Administration building (1935), on Constitution Avenue.

Italy, ruins of Pompeii (650 BC, in 79 covered by ash), a bronze statue of Apollo in the Temple of Apollo (550 BC), west of the Forum Pompeiorum.

Italy, Naples (Napoli 1500 BC), Castel Nuovo (1282, called Maschio Angioino), in front of Piazza Municipio and the city hall.

USA, The Pilgrims Monument in the center of Provincetown, built with granite between 1907 and 1910, commemorates the first landfall of the Pilgrims in 1620, and the signing in Provincetown Harbor of the Mayflower Compact.

UK, Oxford: From Broad St, looking northwest to Trinity College (1555) buildings (right), and Balliol College (1263, center left).

L2.9 – World Classical Music for age 7, 8, 9 and 10

- Listening to Mozart, Vivaldi, Bach, Hayden, Verdi, Rossini, etc.
- Musical instruments
- Singing together
- Mathematics and music
- Music notation
- Beat and rhythm

Recommended books from the Bibliography of this book:
- The City of Light – Paris (La Ville-Lumière) - A kaleidoscopic photographic presentation
- Vivaldi, Bach, Mozart, and Verdi, A chronological and photographic documentary
- Sutherland to Pavarotti: Great Singers History - A chronological and photographic documentary

L'Opéra de Paris (or L'Académie Nationale de Musique, or l'Opéra Garnier, or Le Palais Garnier, or L'Opéra), a 1,979-seat opera house, built from 1861 to 1875, now mainly used for ballet.

Paris: On the façade of l'Opéra de Paris (1875): a statue and the bust of Giovanni Battista Pergolese (or Pergolesi) (1710 -1736), Italian composer, violinist and organist, who wrote La Serva padrona (1733), Il prigioner superbo (1733), Lo frate 'nnamorato (1732), L'Olimpiade (1735), Il Flaminio (1735), Stabat Mater (1736). Johann Sebastian Bach used some of Pergolose's compositions.

Japan, north-west of the Sendai Station (1887), on Ekimae Dori, the restaurant Rigoletto, named after the famous opera with the same name, by Giuseppe Verdi (1813 – 1901), who wrote 37 operas, Rigoletto being the 17th, with the premiere at Teatro La Fenice, Venezia, on 11 March 1851.

USA, University of California, Berkeley (1868), 21 Dec. 2014, il Campanile (1914), some of the 61 bells (full concert carillon).

UK: The program by Candlelight at St Martin in the Fields, on Friday, October 14, 2016 at 7:30 PM, with Antonio Vivaldi (1678 in Venice-1741 (age 63) Vienna), Johann Sebastian Bach (1685-1750 (age 65)), Francesco Geminiani (1687-1762 (age 75)), George Frideric Handel (1685 Germany-1759 (age 74) London UK, buried at Westminster Abbey), Wolfgang Amadeus Mozart (1756 Salzburg, Austria-1791 (age 35) Vienna, Austria), Johann Pachelbel (1653 Nuremberg, Germany-1706 (age 53) Nuremberg, Germany).

UK, London: The Royal Albert Hall (1867-1871, 2004)– an Italian style concert hall on Kensington Gore, on the northern edge of South Kensington, capacity 5,272 seats, 41 m height, named after Prince Consort Albert (1819 (in Germany)-1861), husband (1840-1861) of Queen Victoria (1819-1901, Queen 1837-1901, had 9 children), Chancellor of the University of Cambridge from 1847. In July 1871, French composer Camille Saint-Saëns (1835-1921) performed *Church Scene* from the Faust by Charles Gounod (1818-1893)

L2.10 – Health, Physical Education & Civilized Sport for age 7, 8, 9 and 10

- Self-care
- Washing
- Good food
- Dental care
- Stay clean
- Self discipline
- Be optimist
- Gymnastics
- Ball play
- Circle play
- Running
- Jumping
- Dance
- Basketball
- World football (called soccer in U.S.)

Recommended books from the Bibliography of this book:
- From America to Europe via Japan - A kaleidoscopic photographic documentary
- Discover America and Japan - A photographic documentary
- World Humor History with over 100 Jokes, a new perspective - A chronological and photographic documentary

USA, Tewksbury (settled 1637, incorporated 1734, named after Tewkesbury, England, 31 km northwest of Boston): a golf course

USA, Boston, 2 July 2015, Massachusetts General Hospital (MGH, 1811, the southern façade of the main entrance of the old building).

Switzerland, Geneva (121 BC under Romans), Avenue de la Paix 19, International Committee of the Red Cross founded by Jean Henri Dunant (1828-1910) on Feb. 9, 1863, three Nobel Peace Prizes.

L2.11 – Optional local or other language for age 7, 8, 9 and 10

If a school is in India, for example, the parents could choose Indian or French for their children.

Recommended books from the Bibliography of this book:
- Beautiful Places on Earth – A new photographic presentation

USA, Washington (1790), National Gallery of Art (1937, National Mall)

5 – Secondary: age 11, 12 and 13

4 – The subjects for the Level 3 Secondary:
L3.1 – World Language Mundo based on English
L3.2 – Mathematics
L3.3 – Science & Medicine
L3.4 – Computers & Technology
L3.5 – Art & Practical Work
L3.6 – World and local Geography
L3.7 – World Citizenship & Economics
L3.8 – World and local History of Peace
L3.9 – World Classical Music
L3.10 – Health, Physical Education & Civilized Sport
L3.11 – Optional local or other language

France, Paris: Monument to Alfred de Musset (1810 – 1857, dramatist) in Parc Monceau, (1779, 8.2 ha), on Boulevard de Courcelles.

L3.1 – World Language Mundo based on English for age 11, 12 and 13

- Speaking Mundo
- Reading in Mundo
- Writing in Mundo
- Grammar
- Examples
- Vocabulary development
- Practice
- using only peace oriented secondary level books in Mundo (or English)

Recommended books from the Bibliography of this book:
- Grand Canal – Venice. A new photographic viewpoint. A short presentation with many photos
- Roma (Rome) - La Città Eterna. A new photographic view. A short presentation with many photos
- Rome and Tokyo – two captivating cities. A short photographic presentation
- Paris (Lutetia Parisiorum) – the romance capital of the world - A kaleidoscopic photographic view
- London, Oxford and Cambridge, A photographic documentary
- Vergilius, Horatius, Ovidius, and Shakespeare, A chronological and photographic documentary.
- Socrates to Churchill - Aphorisms celebrated after 1960 - A chronological and photographic documentary

The Institut de France (1795, initially in Louvre, moved in 1805 by Napoléon in this baroque building finished in 1684, for Collège des Quatre-Nations) is a revered French cultural society which includes five académies, the most famous being Académie française (1635) and. Académie des sciences (Academy of Sciences), founded in 1666. The Institute, located on Quai de Conti, manages about 1,000 foundations, as well as museums and châteaux. Its Mazarine Library is France's oldest public library.

USA, San Francisco (1776, on the north tip of a peninsula, near the Pacific Ocean (west) and San Francisco Bay (east)), the northeast part of the Golden Gate Park (1870, 4.1 km^2), the bronze and stone sculpture (1916) Miguel de Cervantes (1547 – 1616) Memorial, with Don Quijote (right down) and Sancho Panza (left down), by Jo Mora (1876 – 1947). In 1605 Cervantes publishes first part of The Ingenious Gentleman Don Quijote of La Mancha, second part in 1615. Cervantes is the father of the modern novel, and his book is one of the most widely read and translated books in the world.

USA, New York, on 5th Ave, the southeast façade of the New York Public Library (1902).

USA, Hammond Castle, 1926-1929, by inventor (400 patents) John Hays Hammond, Jr. (1888-1965), as his home and laboratory, on 7 acres on the Atlantic coast in the Magnolia area of Gloucester.

L3.2 – Mathematics for age 11, 12 and 13

- usual secondary mathematics, including
- numerical calculation
- arithmetic
- geometry
- algebra
- statistics
- measurement

Recommended books from the Bibliography of this book:
- From the USA and Canada to Italy and Japan - A fresh photographic presentation
- 200 Wonderful Places, In The Last 50 Years – A personal photographic documentary

Chicago, 1837: Café Descartes (1596 – 1650, French philosopher, mathematician and writer) on North Michigan Ave.

USA, Cambridge, 1 Feb 2010, geometrical shapes presented at MIT Mathematics Department, including octahedrons (left up, with 8 faces, 12 edges and 6 vertices; a regular octahedron has equilateral triangles for its faces, and is one of the 5 platonic solids), dodecahedrons (with 12 faces, 30 edges and 20 vertices; a regular dodecahedron has regular pentagons for its faces, and is one of the 5 platonic solids), icosahedron (with 20 faces, 30 edges and 12 vertices; all the faces are triangles; a regular icosahedron is one of the 5 platonic solids with all faces being equilateral triangles).

USA, Cleveland, Ohio, in 1983 – M. Dediu (father, right) and Horațiu Dediu (son, left, writing a mathematical proof), at Case Western Reserve University.

Japan, Sendai, the Mathematical Institute at Tohoku University (founded in 1907, the third oldest Imperial University in Japan).

L3.3 – Science & Medicine for age 11, 12 and 13

Usual secondary science and medicine, including:
- Anatomy
- Healthy living habits
- Personal hygiene
- Food
- Air
- Weather
- Plants and animals
- The life cycle
- Light, reflections and refraction, and the way the human eye works.
- The Earth, Sun, Moon, temperature, and melting
- Physics
- Chemical reactions
- Learning about the world and how it works
- World Space Week – celebrating science and technology – in the second week of October. It should be extended for many more weeks.

Recommended books from the Bibliography of this book:
- From the USA and Canada to Italy and Japan - A fresh photographic presentation
- From America to Europe via Japan - A kaleidoscopic photographic documentary
- London and Greenwich, A photographic documentary
- Hippocrates to Fleming: Medicine History celebrated after 1943 - A chronological and photographic documentary
- Pythagoras to Fermi: History of Science - A chronological and photographic documentary

86 Our Future Depends on Good World Education

Japan, Kyoto, 678 (it was the imperial capital of Japan for over 1,000 years): 2 rainbows (center and center-right, over Hitachi) on the east part of Kyoto.

USA, University of California, Berkeley (1868), the Lawrence Hall of Science (1968, public science center mostly for students, with hands-on science exhibits, programs for schools, etc.).

Japan, 20 Nov 2008, in the Ripple Mark Museum, a slice from a 840 years old (from 1110) Cryptomeria japonica conifer, from 1950, with white marks for every 100 years of growth, in Tsukuba Science City (1962), in Ibaraki Prefecture, 60 km north-east of Tokyo.

UK, Greenwich: Peter Harrison (born 1937) Planetarium (2007, 120-seat digital laser planetarium), to the right Main Entrance, The Meridian Line, Flamsteed House (1676), Meridian Observatory.

L3.4 – Computers & Technology for age 11, 12 and 13

- Computer parts names
- How to use a computer
- Playing with a computer
- Start programming
- Computer games

Recommended books from the Bibliography of this book:
- Rome and Tokyo – two captivating cities. A short photographic presentation
- From USA to Japan via Canada – A cheerful photographic documentary
- Three Great Professors: President Woodrow Wilson, Historian Germán Arciniegas, Mathematician Gheorghe Vrănceanu, A chronological and photographic documentary
- From Euclid to Edison - revelries in the last 75 years - A chronological and photographic documentary
- Archimedes to Ford: Invention History celebrated after 1943 - A chronological and photographic documentary

Japan, Tsukuba: HyperMirror – a video camera is on the center-right, and the image is displayed on a high-resolution screen, appearing like a mirror, in a Science Museum in Tsukuba Science City (1962), in Ibaraki Prefecture, 60 km north-east of Tokyo.

USA, Worcester, 23 Jan 2010, the north of the east façade of the Stoddard Laboratories of Worcester Polytechnic Institute (1865).

L3.5 – Art & Practical Work for age 11, 12 and 13

- Classical paintings and sculptures
- Learning to use some painting tools, etc.
- Drawing
- Painting
- Self-care
- Cooking
- Ceramics
- Printmaking
- color theory
- Prepare gifts

Recommended books from the Bibliography of this book:
- Piazza San Marco – Venice. A different photographic view. A short presentation with many photos
- Why is Rome so Fascinating? A short presentation with many photos
- Rome, Boston and Helsinki. A short photographic presentation
- Beautiful Places on Earth – A new photographic presentation
- Paris (Lutetia Parisiorum) – the romance capital of the world - A kaleidoscopic photographic view
- From Berkeley to Pompeii via Rome – A kaleidoscopic photographic documentary
- Da Vinci, Michelangelo, Rembrandt, Rodin - A chronological and photographic documentary

USA, Boston: On the Boston Fan Pier, looking south-west to the Institute of Contemporary Art (left), One Marina Park Drive building (right).

USA, New York (1624): on 42nd street, close to 8th Avenue, inside a tall building, three sculptures of people waiting at a door.

Finland, Helsinki in 2013: the central part of the Ateneum (1885 - 1887, a major museum of classical art). Up a phrase in Latin: Concordia res parvae crescund (By unity small states flourish). The four caryatids represent architecture, painting, music and sculpting.

France, Paris: The statue Cérès ou L'Été (1726) by Coustou Guillaume Lyon (1677 – 1746), placed in 1735 on the east side of the Basin Octogonal in Jardin des Tuileries (created in 1564)

Japan, Chiba Newtown (35 km northeast of Tokyo Imperial Palace, 24 km west of Narita Airport), Alcazar Theater (200 m northeast of Chiba Newtown Chuo Station on Hokuso Line)

USA, San Francisco (1776, on the north tip of a peninsula, near the Pacific Ocean (west) and San Francisco Bay (east)), the northeast part of the Golden Gate Park (1870, 4.1 km^2), the bronze sculpture The Cider Press, by the American sculptor Thomas Shields Clarke (1860 – 1920, educated at Princeton University), originally exhibited at the California Midwinter International Exposition in 1894.

L3.6 – World and local Geography for age 11, 12 and 13

- Globes and maps, projections
- Continents
- Oceans
- Mountains
- Rivers
- Roads
- Bridges
- Cities
- Parks
- Canals
- Comparing, describing,
- Satellite images

Recommended books from the Bibliography of this book:
- Rome, Boston and Helsinki. A short photographic presentation
- From Niagara Falls to Mount Fuji via Rome - A novel photographic presentation
- From the USA and Canada to Italy and Japan - A fresh photographic presentation

Finland, Helsinki: A colorful and elegant building in the center of Helsinki, with Aleksi 13 store, on Mannerheimintie and Esplanadi.

Japan: the north side of Mount Fuji (3,776 m, 1707 last eruption) seen from a hotel window in Kawaguchi city, near Kawaguchiko.

Italy, Roma (753 BC, one of the oldest occupied cities in Europe, called Roma Aeterna (The Eternal City) and Caput Mundi (Capital of the World)), southeast of Piazza del Popolo (1822, by Giuseppe Valadier, inside the northern gate in the Aurelian Walls, the Porta Flaminia, now called the Porta del Popolo), near Via del Babuino (opened in 1525 as the Via Paolina) and the church Santa Maria in Montesanto (1679, begun by Rainaldi and completed by Bernini and Fontana), the statue of the Goddess of Abundance.

Japan, Kobe (201, 30 km west of Osaka), Kobe Port Tower (left, 1963, 108 m, 90 m deck), and Hotel Okura Kobe (right).

France, Chamonix, entrance from France in Mont Blanc tunnel (1959-1965, 11.6 km, 8.6 m by 4.35 m, elevation 1274 m) on 21 Oct 2015, 9:43 AM. The highway tunnel links Chamonix, Haute-Savoie, France with Courmayeur, Aosta Valley, Italy, via European route E25.

Italy, 28 Sep 2008, International Festival with Scottish Bagpipers in Piazza Bra, Verona (Roman Colonia in 89 BC, municipium 49 BC).

UK, London: The entrance of The British Museum (1753), exhibition "Sunken cities, Egypt's lost worlds, 19 May – 27 Nov 2016.

L3.7 – World Citizenship & Economics for age 11, 12 and 13

- World
- One big family
- Follow rules
- Discipline
- Respect your parents and others
- Trustworthy
- Volunteer
- Honesty
- Modesty
- Help others
- Take responsibility for your actions
- Be informed
- Be compassionate
- Be a good neighbor
- Do not make noise
- Be polite
- Speak nicely
- Examples
World Constitution

- Work and Profit
- Finance
- Utility
- Individual Wealth
- World Wealth
- Democracy
- Rights and responsibilities

Recommended books from the Bibliography of this book:
- Beautiful Places on Earth – A new photographic presentation
- Our Future is Sustainable Peace and Prosperity – Moving from conflicts to harmony and peace

USA, New York: W 42nd Street, near 8th Avenue, with the Chrysler Building (1930, 320 m, 77 floors, center-right far back).

USA, Osgood-Pell House, 1888, (William H. Osgood (1830-1896)), from 1992 office for The Preservation Society of Newport County.

L3.8 – World and local History of Peace for age 11, 12 and 13

- Antiquity and peace
- Middle Ages and peace
- Modern time and peace
- Examples
- Analysis

Recommended books from the Bibliography of this book:
- Roma (Rome) - La Città Eterna. A new photographic view. A short presentation with many photos
- 200 Wonderful Places, In The Last 50 Years – A personal photographic documentary
- World History, a new perspective - A chronological and photographic documentary

Italy, Rome: Trajan's column (113, center-left), la Chiesa Santissimo Nome di Maria al Foro Traiano. The columns were part of Basilica Ulpia.

Italy, Roma in 2011: Pantheon (126 AD) and the Fontana del Pantheon in Piazza della Rotonda. Commissioned in 27 BC by Marcus Agrippa (63 BC -12 BC), and rebuilt by Emperor Hadrian (76–138, Emperor 117-138), in about 126.

Japan, north of Hiroshima (1589) Peace Park (1954), Bell of Peace (Sep 20, 1964), the surface of the bell is a map of the world, and the "sweet spot" is an atomic symbol, designed by Masahiko Katori (1899-1988). The Greek inscription on the bell is Socrates' (469 BC – 399 BC) aphorism "Know yourself".

Switzerland, Geneva (121 BC under Romans, 375 m elevation), United Nations seen from Avenue de la Paix.

A table with the flags of the 44 Allied nations, which attended the United Nations Monetary and Financial Conference in July 1944, in the Gold Room of the Mount Washington Resort (1902).

L3.9 – World Classical Music for age 11, 12 and 13

- Listening to Mozart, Vivaldi, Bach, Hayden, Verdi, Rossini, etc.
- Musical instruments
- Singing together
- Mathematics and music
- Music notation
- Beat and rhythm
- Choral singing

Recommended books from the Bibliography of this book:
- The City of Light – Paris (La Ville-Lumière) - A kaleidoscopic photographic presentation
- Sutherland to Pavarotti: Great Singers History - A chronological and photographic documentary

France, Paris: Monument to Frédéric Chopin (1810-1849, composer) in Parc Monceau (1779, 8.2 ha), on Boulevard de Courcelles.

Paris: On the façade de l'Opéra de Paris (1875): a statue and the bust of Domenico Cimarosa (1749 – 1801), Italian opera composer, who wrote more than 80 operas, including Il matrimonio segreto (1792, written in Vienna, where he was invited by Emperor Leopold II (1747 – 1792); Giuseppe Verdi (1813 – 1901) considered it the model opera buffa), Il maestro di capella (1793), Semiramide (1799), Le astuzie femminili (1794), Le nozze di Lauretta (1797).

France, Lyon, Place de la Comédie, l'Opéra National de Lyon (1831, 1993). At the upper western façade of the Opéra: 8 statues out of the 9 Muses: Euterpe (music), Terpsichore (dance), Thalia (comedy), Erato (lyric poetry), Calliope (epic poetry), Polyhymnia (hymns), Melpomene (tragedy), Clio (history) and the missing Muse is Urania (astronomy). The Opéra maintains its own permanent orchestra, choir, ballet, technical, costume and scenery departments. Preparation for a production starts two years before the first night.

Paris: A sculpture with musicians on the right side of the left outer bay on the façade of l'Opéra de Paris (1875), which is the most famous opera house in the world, and a prestigious symbol of Paris. In interior, the ceiling area, which surrounds the chandelier, contains a new 1964 painting by Marc Chagall, which was installed on a removable frame over the original, and depicts scenes from operas by 14 composers, including, Mozart, Bizet, Verdi and Beethoven.

France, Lyon (43 BC), Place de la Comédie, l'Opéra National de Lyon (1831, 1993). Carmen, Danse, Ballet de L' Opéra de Lyon. L'Arlésienne (The Girl from Arles (a city in the south of France)) was composed by Georges Bizet (1838 – 1875) for the first performance of the play with the same name by Alphonse Daudet (1840 – 1897), on 1 October 1872 in Paris at Théâtre du Vaudeville (1868; in a previous building in the Salle de la Bourse on the Place de la Bourse, in 1852, *La Dame aux camélias* by Alexandre Dumas fils (1824 – 1895) was put on here. For the first time in the era, there were over 100 consecutive performances. Giuseppe Verdi (1813 – 1901) was in the audience at this theatre and wrote *La Traviata* (1853) based on the play) on boulevard des Capucines, at the corner of Rue de la Chaussée-d'Antin (now known as the Gaumont Opéra).

Italy, Milano, 30 Sep 2008, in Piazza della Scala (Largo Antonio Ghiringhelli (1906-1979, left), looking northwest to the southeast façade of Teatro alla Scala (3 August 1778, capacity 2,800).

Japan, Osaka, Opera Studio in a small room in a small house on a small street in Osaka.

L3.10 – Health, Physical Education & Civilized Sport for age 11, 12 and 13

- Self-care
- Washing
- Good food
- Dental care
- Stay clean
- Self discipline
- Be optimist
- Gymnastics
- Ball play
- Circle play
- Running
- Jumping
- Dance
- Basketball
- World football (soccer in U.S.)
- Volleyball

Recommended books from the Bibliography of this book:
- From America to Europe via Japan - A kaleidoscopic photographic documentary
- World Humor History with over 100 Jokes, a new perspective - A chronological and photographic documentary

USA, UC Berkeley (1868), Haas Pavilion (1933, 1999, 11,800 capacity, named after the former chairman of Levi Strauss & Co).

Switzerland, Lausanne (150), Place de la Navigation, Olympic clock: 840 jours 4 heures 31 minutes et 43 secondes jusqu'a la ceremonie d'ouverture des Jeux Olympiques d'hiver in Pyeong Chang, South Korea, 2018.

L3.11 – Optional local or other language for age 11, 12 and 13

If a school is in Russia, for example, the parents could choose Chinese or German for their children.

Recommended books from the Bibliography of this book:
- Paris and Tokyo – a joyful photographic presentation. With a preamble about the Universe

Japan, Kyoto, a bust of Ludwig van Beethoven (1770 in Bonn, Germany – 1827 in Vienna, Austria, very famous German composer) on a balcony of a small house.

Paris: The statue of Pierre Corneille (1606 – 1684, poet and dramatist, the creator of French tragedy (Le Cid, Horace, Cinna, La Place royale), one of the three great 17th century French dramatists, along with Molière (1622 – 1673) and Racine (1639 – 1699)) and Paroisse Saint-Étienne-du-Mont (center, 510, 1222, 1328, 1492-1626) – a Catholic church, north-east of the Panthéon (right), with the tombs of Blaise Pascal (1623 – 1662, mathematician, physicist, philosopher, inventor and writer) and Jean-Baptiste Racine.

6 – High School or Vocational: age 14, 15, 16 and 17

4 – The subjects for the Level 4 High School or Vocational:
L4.1 – World Language Mundo based on English
L4.2 – Mathematics
L4.3 – Science & (Medicine or Nursing)
L4.4 – Computers & (Technology or Vocational 1)
L4.5 – (Art & Practical Work) or Vocational 2
L4.6 – Business collaboration
L4.7 – World Citizenship & (Economics or Vocational 3)
L4.8 – Advanced Mathematics or Vocational 4
L4.9 – Advanced Science or Vocational 5
L4.10 – Health, Physical Education & Civilized Sport
L4.11 – Optional other language

World Centers for High School Teaching should change location every year, with the assistance of the United Nations, and could start, for example, in Vienna, Baku (Azerbaijan), Ottawa (Canada), Ouagadougou (Burkina Faso), Copenhagen (Denmark), Djibouti, Tallinn (Estonia), and Asmara (Eritrea).

L4.1 – World Language Mundo based on English for age 14, 15, 16 and 17

- Speaking Mundo
- Creative writing in Mundo, for connections to real-life situations and problem-solving
- Grammar: punctuation, capitalization, spelling, and usage as well as work on logical thinking, and various modes of composition, including the research paper
- Listening and speaking skills
- Examples
- Greek & Latin Roots
- Vocabulary development
- Composition
- Practice
- reading and comprehending literary works including short stories, nonfiction, poetry, drama, novels, and spoken and visual texts.
- using only peace oriented secondary level books in Mundo (or English)
- format writing through computer technology and word processing

Recommended books from the Bibliography of this book:
- Aphorisms and quotations – with examples and explanations
- Piazza San Marco – Venice. A different photographic view. A short presentation with many photos
- Rome, Boston and Helsinki. A short photographic presentation
- Paris – Why So Many Call This City Mon Amour - A lovely photographic presentation
- Paris (Lutetia Parisiorum) – the romance capital of the world - A kaleidoscopic photographic view
- J. R. Lucas – philosopher on a creative parallel with Plato, An American viewpoint
- Vergilius, Horatius, Ovidius, and Shakespeare, A chronological and photographic documentary.

France, Paris: The Panthéon (1758 - 1790, 83 m height, mausoleum in the Latin Quarter in Paris, modeled on the Pantheon in Rome), seen from Rue Soufflot, near Rue Saint-Jacques. This mausoleum, with the motto: *Aux grands hommes, la patrie reconnaissante* ("To the great men, the grateful homeland"), contains the remains of distinguished French citizens (Voltaire, Rousseau, Victor Hugo, etc.). In 1851, physicist Léon Foucault demonstrated the rotation of the earth by his experiment conducted in the Panthéon, by constructing a 67 m Foucault pendulum beneath the central dome.

France, Paris: A statue of Honoré de Balzac (1799 – 1850), well known French novelist and playwright. "La Comédie humaine" (1848) is his main literary work, which has a sequence of 91 short stories and novels about the French life in the years after the 1815, when the era of Napoleon Bonaparte (1769-1821, emperor of the French1804-1814, 1815, king of Italy 1805-1814) ended. It includes the period of the Bourbon Restoration and July Monarchy.

Oxford philosopher J. R. Lucas (right) and M. Dediu on November 3, 2006, at the International Conference "John Stuart Mill, 1806 – 2006".

USA, Cambridge, 26 Sep 2010, Dante Alighieri (1265-1321, poet, statesman, language theorist) Society of Massachusetts, Italian Cultural Center, on Hampshire Street at Cardinal Medeiros Ave., 800 m north of MIT.

L4.2 – Mathematics for age 14, 15, 16 and 17

- usual high school mathematics, including
- numerical calculation, prime factorization
- arithmetic of negative numbers, integers, rational numbers, real numbers, square roots, percentages
- geometry: angles, triangles, polygons, congruence, similarity, Pythagoras' theorem, circles
- algebra, formulae, translation of simple real-world situations into algebraic expressions, solutions of equations, quadratic equations, matrices
- functions
- graphs
- statistics
- trigonometry
- probability
- measurement
- set language and notation
- pre-calculus
- applications of mathematics

Recommended books from the Bibliography of this book:
- Must see places in USA and Japan - A kaleidoscopic photographic documentary
- Three Great Professors: President Woodrow Wilson, Historian Germán Arciniegas, Mathematician Gheorghe Vrănceanu, A chronological and photographic documentary

Germany (southwest), 1978, Oberwolfach (the district of Ortenau in Baden-Württemberg, elevation 323 m (270 m to 948 m), 465 km southwest of Brunswick, and 375 km southwest of Göttingen, in the central Schwarzwald (Black Forest) on the river Wolf, a tributary of the Kinzig.): Academician Professor Dr. Gheorghe Vranceanu (right) and Dr. Michael Dediu at the entrance to the Mathematisches Forschungsinstitut Oberwolfach (Mathematical Research Institute of Oberwolfach, founded in 1944 by the German mathematician Wilhelm Süss (1895-1958)).

Japan, Sendai, the Mathematical Institute at Tohoku University (1907), explaining some announcements of mathematical conferences and seminars, organized by prestigious Universities.

L4.3 – Science & (Medicine or Nursing) for age 14, 15, 16 and 17

Usual high school science and medicine or nursing including:
- Anatomy
- Physiology
- Genetics
- Personal hygiene
- Food
- Air
- Weather: atmosphere
- States and structure of matter
- The life cycle
- Light, reflections and refraction, and the way the human eye works.
- The Earth, Sun, Moon, temperature, and melting
- Physics: atoms, motion, forces, gravity, Newton's laws, energy, waves, sound, light
- Inorganic chemistry
- Botany
- Astronomy
- Stress management
- World Space Week – celebrating science and technology – in the second week of October. It should be extended for many more weeks.

The nursing option will emphasize first aid, patient care, dental assisting, hematology and related subjects.

Recommended books from the Bibliography of this book:
- Rome and Tokyo – two captivating cities. A short photographic presentation
- Grandeurs of the World - A kaleidoscopic photographic documentary
- Hippocrates to Fleming: Medicine History celebrated after 1943 - A chronological and photographic documentary

USA, Boston (1630): Charles River (with the water flowing from left to right, into the Atlantic Ocean (2 km to the east)), Boston (down, Lederman Park) and Cambridge (up, with the Rowland Institute for Science (left, 1980, in 2002 merged with Harvard University, dedicated to experimental research in physics, chemistry and biology (microbial evolution and toxicology)), on the Cambridge Parkway, Charles Park (center left)).

Japan, Tsukuba: Photographs and a layout of the High Energy Accelerator (center-left), at the High Energy Accelerator Research Organization (KEK, 1997) in Tsukuba Science City (1962), in Ibaraki Prefecture, 60 km north-east of Tokyo,

USA, UC Berkeley (1868), the west façade of the Hearst Memorial Mining Building (1907), Engineering, Material Sciences.

USA, Boston, 3 Dec 2009, Massachusetts College of Pharmacy and Health Sciences, 1823, Ronald A. Matricaria Academic and Student Center.

3 Dec 2009, the northeast façade of the Harvard Medical School, Anno Domini 1904, founded in 1782, the graduate medical school of Harvard University (7,200 undergraduates; 14,000 Graduates, 4,671 Faculty members; 152 Nobel laureates are members of Harvard University, 12 Schools and 2 Institutes for Advanced Studies, including Harvard School of Engineering and Applied Sciences, $32.3 billion endowment. $4.2 billion budget).

UK, Greenwich: On Gagarin (First Man in Space) Terrace, on the southwest part of the South Building (1899) of Royal Observatory Greenwich (1676), looking to the south part of the west side (right), the west part of the south side (left), and to the statue of Yuri Gagarin (1934-1968, Russian cosmonaut, the first man to journey into space, with Vostok spacecraft, which completed an orbit (1h 48') of the Earth on 12 April 1961. Resting place: Kremlin Wall Necropolis).

L4.4 – Computers & (Technology or Vocational 1) for age 14, 15, 16 and 17

- Word Processing
- Web design
- More programming
- Computer games
- Information technology

Examples of vocational:
- carpentry
- culinary arts
- electrician
- truck driver
- medical records technician
- emergency medical technician
- plumbing
- office secretaryship
- auto mechanics
- stenography
- marketing
- banking
- metal work
- retail

Recommended books from the Bibliography of this book:
- Beautiful Placcs on Earth – A new photographic presentation
- From USA to Japan via Canada – A cheerful photographic documentary
- Three Great Professors: President Woodrow Wilson, Historian Germán Arciniegas, Mathematician Gheorghe Vrănceanu, A chronological and photographic documentary
- From Euclid to Edison - revelries in the last 75 years - A chronological and photographic documentary
- Archimedes to Ford: Invention History celebrated after 1943 - A chronological and photographic documentary

Washington, D.C. (1790): the Saturn 5 (1967-1973) aft end, at The National Air and Space Museum (1976) of the Smithsonian Institution, between Jefferson Dr SW and Independence Ave SW.

USA, 23 Sep 2009, from Memorial Drive in Cambridge, looking northwest to the MIT (MASSACHVSETTS INSTITVTE OF TECHNOLOGY (in Latin style, with V for U)), MCMXVI (1916).

France, Paris: La Seine, on Parisis boat, looking upstream to the left bank: Port de Suffren with Vedettes de Paris Croisières (Cruises), near Quai Branly, the north-west and south-west sides of la Tour Eiffel (1889, 324 m, 279 m at the 3rd level observatory), with pilier nord on the left, pilier est on the center left back, pilier vest on the center front, and pilier sud on the right.

Japan: a wind turbine 150 m west from the north-east entrance of the Inzai campus of Tokyo Denki University (a private university founded in 1907, and chartered as a university in 1949), 35 km north-east of Tokyo Imperial Palace, 24 km west of Narita International Airport.

21 December 2014, UC Berkeley, Electrical Engineering and Computer Sciences Department in Cory Hall (1950, named for Clarence L. Cory, dean of the College of Mechanics, and a faculty member for almost 40 years. Cory added a fifth floor in 1985. On the exterior, up, a computer chip-inspired design motif. Inside electronic micro-fabrication facility and labs for integrated circuits, lasers, and robotics), north-east corner of campus, on Hearst Av.

L4.5 – (Art & Practical Work) or Vocational 2 for age 14, 15, 16 and 17

Classical paintings and sculptures
- Learning to use some painting tools, etc.
- Drawing
- Painting
- Self-care
- Cooking
- Ceramics
- Printmaking
- Color theory
- Prepare gifts
- Work and Profit
- Finance
- Utility
- Individual Wealth
- World Wealth
- Democracy
- Rights and responsibilities

Examples of vocational:
- carpentry
- culinary arts
- electrician
- truck driver
- medical records technician
- emergency medical technician
- plumbing
- office secretaryship
- auto mechanics
- stenography
- marketing
- banking
- railroad
- boats

- retail

Recommended books from the Bibliography of this book:
- Piazza San Marco – Venice. A different photographic view. A short presentation with many photos
- Grandeurs of the World - A kaleidoscopic photographic documentary
- Da Vinci, Michelangelo, Rembrandt, Rodin - A chronological and photographic documentary

Italy, Venice: A shop window on Riva Longa on San Donato Island, with splendid art glass and glass jewelry.

France, Paris: Musée du Louvre (1793): a statue representing art, in front of Pavillion Richelieu, in Cour Napoléon (1803). The Louvre is located on the right bank of La Seine, in the 1st arrondissement, and has about 35,000 museum objects, exhibited over an area of 60,600 m^2. With more than 8 million visitors each year, the Louvre is the world's most visited museum. The museum is housed in the Palais du Louvre, originally built as a fortress around 1190 under Philip II of France (1165 – 1223, king 1179 – 1223).

Japan, Tokyo, Ginza: Kabuki Za Theatre on Harumi Dori (over No. 2 Hibiya Line) at the corner with Showa Dori (over No. 1 Asakusa Line). This is the principal theatre in Tokyo for the traditional kabuki drama. It has a capacity of 1964 spectators, was built in 1889, rebuilt in 1911, 1924, 1950 and 2013. Kabuki is an over 400 years old classical Japanese dance-drama, with high stylization, elaborate make-up, and a sophisticated art of singing and dancing.

Italy, Rome (753 BC), Piazza Colonna, the northwest side of The Doric Column (193, 40 m, 27 blocks of Carrara marble, diameter 3.78 m, stairway of 200 steps within) of Marcus Aurelius (Latin: *Columna Centenaria Divorum Marci et Faustinae*), with a spiral relief: it was built in honor of Roman emperor and one of the most important Stoic philosophers Marcus Aurelius (121 – 180, joint 16th emperor 161 – 180, regarding the triumph over the Marcomanni, Quadi and Sarmatians in the year 176), and modeled on Trajan's Column. (113, 35 m, Traianus (53–117)).

Japan, Hiroshima (means "wide island", 1589, Hiroshima Castle built in 1593, Ujina Harbor built in 1885, the Sanyo Railway extended to Hiroshima in 1894, Emperor Meiji (1852 – 1912) maintained his headquarters at Hiroshima Castle in 1894 – 1895, on Honshu Island, current population about 1.2 million), on Aioi Dori, a book statue near Mizuho Bank Hiroshima Branch, 500 m east of Hiroshima Peace Memorial Park.

L4.6 – Business collaboration for age 14, 15, 16 and 17

- Entrepreneurship
- E-commerce
- Accounting

Recommended books from the Bibliography of this book:
- Piazza San Marco – Venice. A different photographic view. A short presentation with many photos
- The City of Light – Paris (La Ville-Lumière) - A kaleidoscopic photographic presentation
- 200 Wonderful Places, In The Last 50 Years – A personal photographic documentary

Bourse de Paris in Palais Brongniart (1808 – 1826, by Napoleon), seen through Rue de la Bourse, from Rue de Richelieu.

Italy, Venice: Universita Ca' Foscari di Venezia, on Fondamenta di San Giobbe, at the north-west entrance of Canale di Cannaregio, on the north-west part of Venezia. Ca' Foscari University of Venice was founded in 1868, as the first Italian business college.

The main seat of the University is Ca' Foscari Palace, the Venetian Gothic building placed in the largest bend of the Grand Canal. The palace was purchased and renewed by Doge Francesco Foscari in 1452. It contains important artistic and architectural works, such as: a room with a 15th century frescoed floor and a 16th century decorated roof; a room with a 16th century stucco work by the Venetian sculpture Alessandro Vittoria (1525-1608); a great hall designed by the Venetian architect Carlo Scarpa (1906-1978), with two murals by Mario Sironi and Mario de Luigi.

Ca' Foscari participates actively in the city's cultural life, organizing over 400 events every year. The University holds successful art exhibitions in "Ca' Foscari Esposizioni", the exhibition space in the main building. Ca' Foscari also offers nine Summer Schools including the prestigious Ca' Foscari - Harvard Summer School, the result of a bilateral agreement between Ca' Foscari and the American university.

L4.7 – World Citizenship & (Economics or Vocational 3) for age 14, 15, 16 and 17

- World
- One big family
- Follow rules
- Discipline
- Respect your parents and others
- Trustworthy
- Volunteer
- Honesty
- Modesty
- Help others
- Take responsibility for your actions
- Be informed
- Be compassionate
- Be a good neighbor
- Do not make noise
- Be polite
- Speak nicely
- World Constitution:
    - rules
    - small World Government
    - elections
    - advisors' levels
    - assistants
    - administrators
    - Honorific Word Observer
    - medical assistance
    - people assistance services
    - total disarmament
    - no conflicts
    - no war
    - no military forces
    - no arms
    - no abuses

　　　　　- freedom and responsibility
　　　　　- census
　　　　　- special credit card
　　　　　- World Central Bank
　　　　　- new world currency
　　　　　- budgets with surplus
　　　　　- no borrowing
　　　　　- International standards
　　　　　- World Post Offices
　　　　　- free commerce
　　　　　- prevention first
　　　　　- language and alphabet

- Work and Profit
- Finance
- Utility
- Individual Wealth
- World Wealth
- Democracy
- Rights and responsibilities

Examples of vocational:
- carpentry
- culinary arts
- electrician
- truck driver
- medical records technician
- emergency medical technician
- plumbing
- office secretaryship
- auto mechanics
- stenography
- marketing
- banking
- retail

Recommended books from the Bibliography of this book:
- 100 Great Personalities and their Quotations

- Paris – Why So Many Call This City Mon Amour - A lovely photographic presentation
- 200 Wonderful Places, In The Last 50 Years – A personal photographic documentary
- Our Future is Sustainable Peace and Prosperity – Moving from conflicts to harmony and peace

France, Paris: On the north side of the Avenue des Champs-Élysées, a red Ferrari supercar from Ferrari S.p.A. (1929, 1947, in Maranello, Italy).

Paris: On the façade of l'Opéra de Paris (1875): a statue and the bust of Johann Sebastian Bach (1685 – 1750), one of the greatest German composers and organists, who wrote the Branderburg Concertos, the Well-Tempered Clavier, over 200 cantatas, two Passions, and keyboard works. Mozart, Beethoven, Chopin, Schumann and Mendelssohn were admirers of Bach. Beethoven described him as the "Urvater der Harmonie" (the original father of harmony).

Italy: Roma in 2011: Trajan's column was erected in 113 AD in honor of Emperor Trajan. It is located at the Forum of Trajan, near Piazza Venezia and Altare della Patria. The column commemorates Trajan's victories in Dacia (now Romania), and it is 42 meters tall, including its base.

Japan, 17 April 2015, center of the Hiroshima (1589) Peace Memorial Park (1954), with the Peace Clock Tower (right up).

USA, the room in the Mount Washington Resort, Bretton Woods, New Hampshire, USA, where the documents of the United Nations Monetary and Financial Conference were signed in July 1944.

L4.8 – Advanced Mathematics or Vocational 4 for age 14, 15, 16 and 17

- coordinate geometry
- vectors
- binomial expansions
- solving simple equations involving exponential, logarithmic and modulus functions
- calculus
- application of differentiation and integration to problems involving displacement, velocity and acceleration of a particle moving in a straight line with variable or constant acceleration

Examples of vocational:
- carpentry
- culinary arts
- electrician
- truck driver
- medical records technician
- emergency medical technician
- plumbing
- office secretaryship
- auto mechanics
- stenography
- marketing
- banking
- retail

Recommended books from the Bibliography of this book:
- Paris (Lutetia Parisiorum) – the romance capital of the world - A kaleidoscopic photographic view
- Three Great Professors: President Woodrow Wilson, Historian Germán Arciniegas, Mathematician Gheorghe Vrănceanu, A chronological and photographic documentary

France, Paris: Bust of Alexandre Gustave Eiffel (1832 – 1923) at the foot of Tour Eiffel (1889, 324 m, 279 m 3rd level). Eiffel also built over 60 buildings, structures, bridges and viaducts, including Railway station at Toulouse, France (1862), Théâtre les Folies, Paris (1868), Cathedral of San Pedro de Tacna, Peru (1875), Eiffel Bridge in Ungheni, Romania (1877), Grand Hotel Traian, Iași, Romania (1882), Garabit Viaduct, France (1884), Statue of Liberty, Liberty Island, New York, United States (1886).

2 May 1977, Fribourg (40,000 inhabitants), Switzerland, Mathematishes Institut or Département de mathématiques (the Faculty of Mathematics and Science was founded in 1896), Université de Fribourg (founded in 1889 by Georges Python (1856-1927), the only bilingual (French and German) university in Switzerland, five faculties, 10,000 students, 800 faculty), Chemin du Musée 23, close to the river La Sarine.

UK, Cambridge University Press: Entropy, Lagrangians and Hamiltonians, Statistics Explained, Quantum Field Theory

L4.9 – Advanced Science or Vocational 5 for age 14, 15, 16 and 17

- Biology
- Zoology
- Anthropology

Examples of vocational:
- carpentry
- culinary arts
- electrician
- truck driver
- medical records technician
- emergency medical technician
- plumbing
- office secretaryship
- auto mechanics
- stenography
- marketing
- banking
- glass work
- retail

Recommended books from the Bibliography of this book:
- Axioms, aphorisms and quotations – with examples and explanations
- Why is Rome so Fascinating? A short presentation with many photos
- 200 Wonderful Places, In The Last 50 Years – A personal photographic documentary
- Pythagoras to Fermi: History of Science - A chronological and photographic documentary

Japan, Tsukuba, 20 Nov 2008, inside the main research building, photographs with celebrity physicists, like Galileo Galilei (1564 – 1642, who used the Leaning Tower of Pisa, Italy (1173 – 1372), center-right), at the High Energy Accelerator Research Organization (KEK, 1997) in Tsukuba Science City (1962), in Ibaraki Prefecture, 60 km north-east of Tokyo,

Our Future Depends on Good World Education 153

The campus Città Universitaria (1935) of Sapienza – Università di Roma (1303), 2.5 km north-east of Colosseum, 140,000 students

France, Paris: A Lamborghini supercar (Automobili Lamborghini, 1963, Italy), in the east part of Place de la Concorde, near Tuileries Gardens.

Italy, Venezia, Murano in 2012: a beautiful Murano glass sculpture in Murano Square. Some of the companies that own historical glass factories in Murano are Venini, Ferro Murano, Barovier & Toso, Simone Cenedese and Seguso. Pauly & C. – Compagnia Venezia Murano is the oldest Murano glass factory, founded in 1866, which is still active today. The artisans of Murano created milk glass (lattimo), and imitation gemstones made of glass.

Japan, 24 Nov 2008, inside Hyogo Earthquake Engineering Center, the biggest earthquake research center in the world, in Miki City, near Kobe. Buildings tested on the Earthquake Defense shake table.

UK, London's only planetarium bronze cone (the largest in the world, 250 welded plates). The cone is sliced at angle parallel to celestial equator, the line on the slice is north (left, perpendicular) south (up) is parallel to 0 meridian, angle of the southern side (right) is equal to latitude of Royal Observatory Greenwich 51° 22' 44" N.

L4.10 – Health, Physical Education & Civilized Sport for age 14, 15, 16 and 17

- Self-care
- Washing
- Good food
- Dental care
- Stay clean
- Self discipline
- Be optimist
- Gymnastics
- Ball play
- Circle play
- Running
- Jumping
- Dance
- Basketball
- World football (soccer in U.S.)
- Volleyball
- Handball
- Tennis
- Golf

Recommended books from the Bibliography of this book:
- Paris – Why So Many Call This City Mon Amour - A lovely photographic presentation
- 17 Picturesque Cities on the World Map - A photographic documentary
- World Humor History with over 100 Jokes, a new perspective - A chronological and photographic documentary

USA, Boston, 3 Dec 2009, on Longwood Ave, looking northwest to Harvard School of Dental Medicine (1867), 188 Longwood Avenue.

UK, Cambridge: From the south gate of Trinity College (1546) Great Court (which is the main court), looking north to the northern part of the Great Court (the largest enclosed court in Europe).

L4.11 – Optional other language for age 14, 15, 16 and 17

If a school is in the U.S., for example, the parents could choose Russian or Italian for their children.

Recommended books from the Bibliography of this book:
- Roma (Rome) - La Città Eterna. A new photographic view. A short presentation with many photos
- Sutherland to Pavarotti: Great Singers History - A chronological and photographic documentary

UK, Oxford: Oriel College (1326, in the back: the east range of First quadrangle, with ornate portico in the center)).

7 – Education at all levels

7 – Let's emphasize again that education at all levels is important in order to have the young generation leave healthy, in a sustainable peace, liberty and prosperity. Discipline must be strict, and those who do not behave properly, will get medical assistance.

World Centers for Promoting Good Education and Discipline should change location every year, with the assistance of the World Police and Assistance Unit (former United Nations), and could start, for example, in the capitals of the Regions R0,…,R9 mentioned in the book "Sustainable Peace and Prosperity".

Also, all the people working in education should have in mind the following aphorisms:

Rule 28-1: People know very well that *As you sow, so shall you reap* – from Latin: Ut sementem feceris ita metes.

Rule 28-2: Aristotle: The roots of education are bitter, but the fruit is sweet.

Rule 28-3: Plato: Ignorance, the root and stem of all evil.

Rule 28-4: Plato: Let parents bequeath to their children not riches, but the spirit of reverence.

Rule 28-5: Plato: No man should bring children into the world, who is unwilling to persevere to the end in their nature and education.

Rule 28-6: Plato: There is no harm in repeating a good thing.

Rule 28-7: Plato: We ought to esteem it of the greatest importance, that the fictions, which children first hear, should be adapted in the most perfect manner to the promotion of virtue.

Rule 28-8: Beethoven: Recommend to your children virtue; that alone can make them happy, not gold. I speak from experience

Rule 28-9: Cicero: A home without books is a body without soul.

Rule 28-10: Cicero: Cultivation to the mind is as necessary as food to the body.

Rule 28-11: Solon: I grow old learning something new every day.

Rule 28-12: Archimedes: There are things which seem incredible to most men who have not studied Mathematics.

Rule 28-13: Cicero: There are more men ennobled by study than by nature.

Rule 28-14: Cicero: What nobler employment, or more valuable to the state, than that of the man who instructs the rising generation?

Rule 28-14: Cicero: They condemn what they do not understand – from Latin: **Damnant quodnon intelligunt.**

Rule 28-15: Seneca: Men learn while they teach – from Latin: **Homines dum docent discunt.**

Rule 28-16: Quintilian: For the mind is all the easier to teach before it is set.

Rule 28-17: Quintilian: We must form our minds by reading deep rather than wide.

Rule 28-18: Leonardo da Vinci: Learning never exhausts the mind.

Rule 28-19: John Milton: A good book is the precious lifeblood of a master spirit.

Rule 28-20: John Milton: The superior man acquaints himself with many sayings of antiquity and many deeds of the past, in order to strengthen his character thereby.

Rule 28-21: Lambert: I understood that the will could not be improved before the mind had been enlightened.

Rule 28-22: Jefferson: Books constitute capital. A library book lasts as long as a house, for hundreds of years. It is not, then, an article of mere consumption but fairly of capital, and often in the case of professional men, setting out in life, it is their only capital.

Rule 28-23: Goethe: All intelligent thoughts have already been thought; what is necessary is only to try to think them again.

Rule 28-24: Lincoln: Books serve to show a man that those original thoughts of his aren't very new at all.

Rule 28-25: Mark Twain: The man, who doesn`t read good books, has no advantage over the man who can`t read them.

Rule 28-26: Anatole France: An education isn't how much you have committed to memory, or even how much you know. It's being able to differentiate between what you know, and what you don't.

Rule 28-27: Dediu: Few people know,
        How much you have to know,
        To know,
        How little you know.

Rule 28-28: Be hungrier for knowledge than for food.

Rule 28-29: Even a drop of education can change the color of an ocean of ignorance.
Computers are tools for education, not substitutes of it.

Rule 28-30: Newton: I do not know what I may appear to the world; but to myself I seem to have been only like a boy playing on the seashore, and diverting myself now and then finding a smoother pebble or a prettier shell than ordinary, whilst the great ocean of truth lay all undiscovered before me.

Rule 28-31: Voltaire: A human being is not attaining his full heights until he is educated.

Rule 28-32: Descartes: The reading of all good books is like a conversation with the finest minds of past centuries.

Rule 28-33: Confucius: You cannot open a book without learning something.

8 – Science and Technology

8 – It is well known that science and technology play a major role in education, and here are some useful aphorisms:

Rule 29-1: Plato: This City is what it is because our citizens are what they are.

Rule 29-2: Plato: We ought to fly away from Earth to heaven as quickly as we can; and to fly away is to become like God, as far as this is possible; and to become like him is to become holy, just, and wise.

Rule 29-3: Seneca: There is no easy way from the Earth to the stars – Latin: Non est ad astra mollis e terris via.

Rule 29-4: Poincare: It is far better to foresee even without certainty, than not to foresee at all.

Rule 29-5: Data, mathematical modeling and simulations are critical to planning for, and maintaining sustainable communities all over the world.

Rule 29-6: Niels Bohr: Technology has advanced more in the last thirty years than in the previous two thousands. The exponential increase in advancement will only continue.

Rule 29-7: Caesar: Creating is the essence of life.

Rule 29-8: Beethoven: There are not barriers erected, which can say to aspiring talents and industry, "Thus far and no farther."

Rule 29-9: J. S. Mill: All good things which exist are the fruits of originality.

Rule 29-10: All forms of art which help people are welcome.

Rule 29-11: Pasteur: In the field of scientific observation, chance favors only the prepared mind.

Rule 29-12: Cantor: The essence of mathematics lies in its freedom.

Rule 29-13: Clifford: An atmosphere of beliefs and conceptions has been formed by the labors and struggles of our forefathers, which enables us to breathe amid the various and complex circumstances of our life.

Rule 29-14: Clifford: If a belief is not realized immediately in open deeds, it is stored up for the guidance of the future.

Rule 29-15: Clifford: It is wrong always, everywhere, and for anyone, to believe anything upon insufficient evidence.

Rule 29-16: Clifford: No simplicity of mind, no obscurity of station, can escape the universal duty of questioning all that we believe.

Rule 29-17: Poincaré: It is through science that we prove, but through intuition that we discover.

Rule 29-18: Poincaré: Mathematical discoveries, small or great, are never born of spontaneous generation.

Rule 29-19: Poincaré: Mathematicians are born, not made.

Rule 29-20: Poincaré: To doubt everything, or, to believe everything, are two equally convenient solutions; both dispense with the necessity of reflection.

Rule 29-21: Poincaré: One would have to have completely forgotten the history of science, so as to not remember that the desire to know nature has had the most constant, and the happiest influence on the development of mathematics.

Rule 29-22: Whitehead: Civilization advances by extending the number of important operations, which we can perform without thinking of them.

Rule 29-23: Hoover: New discoveries in science will continue to create a thousand new frontiers for those who still would adventure.

Rule 29-24: Picasso: Art washes away from the soul the dust of everyday life.
We don't grow older, we grow riper.
Work is a necessity for man. Man invented the alarm clock.
Youth has no age.

Rule 29-25: Banach: Mathematics is as old as Man.
Mathematics is the most beautiful and most powerful creation of the human spirit.

Rule 29-26: Innovation is applied creativity.

Rule 29-27: Science and technology are the engines of progress.
The Internet is like a huge library – keep it clean and unpolluted.

9 - World Constitution

At different levels of education, some of the following World Constitution subjects will be presented:
- rules
- small World Government, with 7 small departments
- elections - every 20 months for one term only, based on exceptional results, no propaganda
- advisors' levels - minimum age 25 years, First Adviser for one month, by rotation
- assistants
- administrators
- Honorific Word Observer
- medical assistance, Specialized Medical Institutions for disorderly behavior
- people assistance services
- some police with small arms
- total disarmament
- no conflicts
- no war
- no military forces
- no arms
- no abuses
- freedom and responsibility
- people can assemble peacefully only
- census
- special credit card
- World Central Bank
- new world currency
- budgets with surplus
- tax: 15% of income
- no borrowing
- 40 hours/week, compensation
- savings accounts for old age
- International standards
- Intellectual Rights

- World Post Offices
- free commerce and collaboration
- common sense
- prevention of bad events first - if bad, then pay all expense and reimburse
- language and alphabet

Italy, Rome (753 BC), from cordonata capitolina (flight of steps, which can be also used by horses, with balustrades ending down with two Egyptian lions in black basalt, and up with two marble statues of Castor (left) and Pollux (right), by Michelangelo), Campidoglio (1546 by Michelangelo, on Collis Capitolinus, the oldest part of Rome, with Temple of Jupiter, 509 BC), Palazzo Senatorio (back, 1350, atop Tabularium, now the city hall).

10 - Conclusions

10.1 - It is obvious that if all aver 2 B of children on Earth will learn well from the classes presented above, our future will be in good hands!

10.2 - The purpose of education is to give a solid foundation for a good life.

10.3 - The purpose for all over 7.7 B of people on Earth is to be healthy, to live in peace, freedom and harmony, to be prosperous, and to prepare to expand to the Moon, asteroids, Mars, and everywhere else in the Universe.

USA, Ohio, Cleveland, August 1979, NASA John H. Glenn Research Center (1942, near the airport), Agena rochet (1959-1987).

Italy, Venezia - In the middle of the west façade of the Basilica di San Marco, we see the central bronze-fashioned door, in a round-arched portal, encircled by polychrome marble columns. Above this door there are three round bas-relief cycles of Romanesque art. A Japanese couple, with their Japanese photographer, make their wedding photographs in this most beautiful place.

Bibliography

"The Histories" by Polybius
"Discours de la Méthode" by René Descartes
"Meditationes de prima philosophia" by René Descartes
"Philosophiae Naturalis Principia Mathematica" by Isaac Newton
Chinese encyclopedia Gujin Tushu Jicheng (Imperial Enciclopaedia)
"Encyclopédie" by Jean-Baptiste le Rond d'Alembert and Denis Diderot
"Encyclopaedia Britannica" by over 4,400 contributors
"Encyclopedia Americana" by Francis Lieber
"Grand Larousse encyclopédique en 24 volumes" by Albert Ducrocq
Nobel Prize Organization
"The Cambridge History of Medicine", edited by Roy Porter
"Great Russian Encyclopedia" by Yury Osipov
"Encyclopedia of China"
"Enciclopedia Italiana di Scienze, Lettere ed Arti" (35 volume), by Giovanni Treccani
Concise Oxford Dictionary of Opera
"Allgemeine Encyclopädie der Wissenschaften und Künste" by Johann Samuel Ersch und Johann Gottfried Gruber
Grove Dictionary of Music and Musicians
"Gran Enciclopedia de España"
Other sources include: UPI, CNBC, AP, Nasdaq, Reuters, EDGAR, AFP, Recode, Europa Press, Bloomberg News, Fox News, USA, Deutsche Presse-Agentur, MSNBC, BBC, Australian Associated Press, Agência Brasil, The Canadian Press (La Presse Canadienne), Middle East News Agency, Baltic News Service, Suomen Tietotoimisto, Athens-Macedonian News Agency, Asian News International, Inter Press Service, Kyodo News, Notimex, Algemeen Nederlands Persbureau, AGERPRES, Newsis, Tidningarnas Telegrambyrå, Swiss Telegraphic Agency, Central News Agency, ANKA news agency, Agenzia Fides

Michael M. Dediu is also the author of these books (which can be found on Amazon.com):

1. Aphorisms and quotations – with examples and explanations
2. Axioms, aphorisms and quotations – with examples and explanations
3. 100 Great Personalities and their Quotations
4. Professor Petre P. Teodorescu – A Great Mathematician and Engineer
5. Professor Ioan Goia – A Dedicated Engineering Professor
6. Venice (Venezia) – a new perspective. A short presentation with photographs
7. La Serenissima (Venice) - a new photographic perspective. A short presentation with many photos
8. Grand Canal – Venice. A new photographic viewpoint. A short presentation with many photos
9. Piazza San Marco – Venice. A different photographic view. A short presentation with many photos
10. Roma (Rome) - La Città Eterna. A new photographic view. A short presentation with many photos
11. Why is Rome so Fascinating? A short presentation with many photos
12. Rome, Boston and Helsinki. A short photographic presentation
13. Rome and Tokyo – two captivating cities. A short photographic presentation
14. Beautiful Places on Earth – A new photographic presentation
15. From Niagara Falls to Mount Fuji via Rome - A novel photographic presentation
16. From the USA and Canada to Italy and Japan - A fresh photographic presentation
17. Paris – Why So Many Call This City Mon Amour - A lovely photographic presentation
18. The City of Light – Paris (La Ville-Lumière) - A kaleidoscopic photographic presentation
19. Paris (Lutetia Parisiorum) – the romance capital of the world - A kaleidoscopic photographic view
20. Paris and Tokyo – a joyful photographic presentation. With a preamble about the Universe

21. From USA to Japan via Canada – A cheerful photographic documentary
22. 200 Wonderful Places, In The Last 50 Years – A personal photographic documentary
23. Must see places in USA and Japan - A kaleidoscopic photographic documentary
24. Grandeurs of the World - A kaleidoscopic photographic documentary
25. Corneliu Leu – writer on the same wavelength as Mark Twain. An American viewpoint
26. From Berkeley to Pompeii via Rome – A kaleidoscopic photographic documentary
27. From America to Europe via Japan - A kaleidoscopic photographic documentary
28. Discover America and Japan - A photographic documentary
29. J. R. Lucas – philosopher on a creative parallel with Plato, An American viewpoint
30. From America to Switzerland via France - A photographic documentary
31. From Bretton Woods to New York via Cape Cod - A photographic documentary
32. Splendid Places on the Atlantic Coast of the U. S. A. - A photographic documentary
33. Fourteen nice Cities on three Continents - A photographic documentary
34. 17 Picturesque Cities on the World Map - A photographic documentary
35. Unforgettable Places from Four Continents including Trump buildings - A photographic documentary
36. Dediu Newsletter, Volume 1, Number 1, 6 December 2016 – Monthly news, review, comments and suggestions for a better and wiser world
37. Dediu Newsletter, Volume 1, Number 2, 6 January 2017 (available at www.derc.com).
38. Dediu Newsletter, Volume 1, Number 3, 6 February 2017 (available at www.derc.com).
39. London and Greenwich, A photographic documentary
40. Dediu Newsletter, Volume 1, Number 4, 6 March 2017 (available also at www.derc.com).

41. Dediu Newsletter, Volume 1, Number 5, 6 April 2017 (available also at www.derc.com).
42. Dediu Newsletter, Volume 1, Number 6, 6 May 2017 (available also at www.derc.com).
43. Dediu Newsletter, Volume 1, Number 7, 6 June 2017 (available also at www.derc.com).
44. London, Oxford and Cambridge, A photographic documentary
45. Dediu Newsletter, Volume 1, Number 8, 6 July 2017 (available also at www.derc.com).
46. Dediu Newsletter, Volume 1, Number 9, 6 August 2017 (available also at www.derc.com).
47. Dediu Newsletter, Volume 1, Number 10, 6 September 2017 (available also at www.derc.com).
48. Three Great Professors: President Woodrow Wilson, Historian Germán Arciniegas, Mathematician Gheorghe Vrănceanu, A chronological and photographic documentary
49. Dediu Newsletter, Volume 1, Number 11, 6 October 2017 (available also at www.derc.com).
50 Dediu Newsletter, Volume 1, Number 12, 6 November 2017 (available also at www.derc.com).
51 Dediu Newsletter, Volume 2, Number 1 (13), 6 December 2017 (available also at www.derc.com).
52 Two Great Leaders: Augustus and George Washington, A chronological and photographic documentary
53. Dediu Newsletter, Volume 2, Number 2 (14), 6 January 2018 (available also at www.derc.com).
54. Newton, Benjamin Franklin, and Gauss, A chronological and photographic documentary
55. Dediu Newsletter, Volume 2, Number 3 (15), 6 February 2018 (available also at www.derc.com).
56. 2017: World Top Events, But Many Little Known, A chronological and photographic documentary
57. Dediu Newsletter, Volume 2, Number 4 (16), 6 March 2018 (available also at www.derc.com).
58. Vergilius, Horatius, Ovidius, and Shakespeare, A chronological and photographic documentary.
59. Dediu Newsletter, Volume 2, Number 5 (17), 6 April 2018 (available also at www.derc.com).

60. Dediu Newsletter, Volume 2, Number 6 (18), 6 May 2018 (available also at www.derc.com).
61. Vivaldi, Bach, Mozart, and Verdi, A chronological and photographic documentary
62. Dediu Newsletter, Volume 2, Number 7 (19), 6 June 2018 (available also at www.derc.com).
63. Dediu Newsletter, Volume 2, Number 8 (20), 6 July 2018 (available also at www.derc.com).
64. Dediu Newsletter, Volume 2, Number 9 (21), 6 August 2018 (available also at www.derc.com).
65. World History, a new perspective - A chronological and photographic documentary.
66. World Humor History with over 100 Jokes, a new perspective - A chronological and photographic documentary
67. Dediu Newsletter, Vol 2, N 10 (22), 6 September 2018
68. Dediu Newsletter, Vol 2, N 11 (23), 6 October 2018
69. Da Vinci, Michelangelo, Rembrandt, Rodin - A chronological and photographic documentary
70. Dediu Newsletter, Vol 2, N 12 (24), 6 November 2018
71. Dediu Newsletter, Vol 3, N 1 (25), 6 December 2018
72. From Euclid to Edison - revelries in the last 75 years - A chronological and photographic documentary
73. Dediu Newsletter, Vol 3, N 2 (26), 6 January 2019
74. Socrates to Churchill - Aphorisms celebrated after 1960 - A chronological and photographic documentary
75. Dediu Newsletter Vol 3, Number 3 (27), 6 February 2019
76. Hippocrates to Fleming: Medicine History celebrated after 1943 - A chronological and photographic documentary
77. Dediu Newsletter, Volume 3, Number 4 (28), 6 March 2019
78. Dediu Newsletter, Volume 3, Number 5 (29), 6 April 2019
79. Archimedes to Ford: Invention History celebrated after 1943 - A chronological and photographic documentary
80. Dediu Newsletter, Volume 3, Number 6 (30), 6 May 2019
81. Sutherland to Pavarotti: Great Singers History - A chronological and photographic documentary
82. Dediu Newsletter, Volume 3, Number 7 (31), 6 June 2019
83. Dediu Newsletter, Volume 3, Number 8 (32), 6 July 2019
84. Augustus to Rockefeller: History of the Wealthiest People - A chronological and photographic documentary

85. Dediu Newsletter, Volume 3, Number 9 (33), 6 August 2019
86 – Pythagoras to Fermi: History of Science - A chronological and photographic documentary
87. Dediu Newsletter, Volume 3, Number 10 (34), 6 September 2019
88. Our Future is Sustainable Peace and Prosperity – Moving from conflicts to harmony and peace
89 - Dediu Newsletter, Volume 3, Number 11 (35), 6 October 2019 – World Monthly Report with News

USA, Washington: Woodrow Wilson International Center for Scholars (1968) had a meeting regarding the 1913 Centennial, in celebration of the 100th anniversary of President Woodrow Wilson's inauguration.

Michael M. Dediu is the editor of these books (also on Amazon.com):

1. Sophia Dediu: The life and its torrents – Ana. In Europe around 1920
2. Proceedings of the 4th International Conference "Advanced Composite Materials Engineering" COMAT 2012
3. Adolf Shvedchikov: I am an eternal child of spring – poems in English, Italian, French, German, Spanish and Russian
4. Adolf Shvedchikov: Life's Enigma – poems in English, Italian and Russian
5. Adolf Shvedchikov: Everyone wants to be HAPPY – poems in English, Spanish and Russian
6. Adolf Shvedchikov: My Life, My Love – poems in English, Italian and Russian
7. Adolf Shvedchikov: I am the gardener of love – poems in English and Russian
8. Adolf Shvedchikov: Amaretta di Saronno – poems in English and Russian
9. Adolf Shvedchikov: A Russian Rediscovers America
10. Adolf Shvedchikov: Parade of Life - poems in English and Russian
11. Adolf Shvedchikov: Overcoming Sorrow - poems in English and Russian
12. Sophia Dediu: Sophia meets Japan
13. Corneliu Leu: Roosevelt, Churchill, Stalin and Hitler: Their surprising role in Eastern Europe in 1944
14. Proceedings of the 5th International Conference "Computational Mechanics and Virtual Engineering" COMEC 2013
15. Georgeta Simion – Potanga: Beyond Imagination: A Thought-provoking novel inspired from mid-20th century events
16. Ana Dediu: The poetry of my life in Europe and The USA
17. Ana Dediu: The Four Graces
18. Proceedings of the 5th International Conference "Advanced Composite Materials Engineering" COMAT 2014
19. Sophia Dediu: Chocolate Cook Book: Is there such a thing as too much chocolate?

20. Sorin Vlase: Mechanical Identifiability in Automotive Engineering
21. Gabriel Dima: The Evolution of the Aerostructures – Concept and Technologies
22. Proceedings of the 6th International Conference "Computational Mechanics and Virtual Engineering" COMEC 2015
23. Sophia Dediu: Cook Book 1 A-B-C Common sense cooking
24. Sophia Dediu: Dim Sum Spring Festival
25. Ana Dediu and Sophia Dediu: Europe in 1985: A chronological and photographic documentary
26 Stefan Staretu: Europe: Serbian Despotate of Srem and the Romanian area. Between the 14th and the 16th Centuries

Italy, Venezia - The south end of La Piazzetta, the south part of Piazza San Marco, with gondole, and wedding pictures of a Japanese couple.

www.ingramcontent.com/pod-product-compliance
Lightning Source LLC
Chambersburg PA
CBHW041609220426
43667CB00001B/10